BREAK THROUGH

To Wendy

Thanks for always being
such a blessing
Lots of love
Mark Pennell

MARK FENNELL is a high-performance life coach and mentor with a 20-year track record, renowned for his deep understanding of the human mind, psychology and performance. He has worked with many top global corporations, individuals and teams. He appears regularly on major TV and radio networks in Ireland and the UK and has worked with the BBC, RTÉ, Virgin Media and Newstalk.

BREAK THROUGH

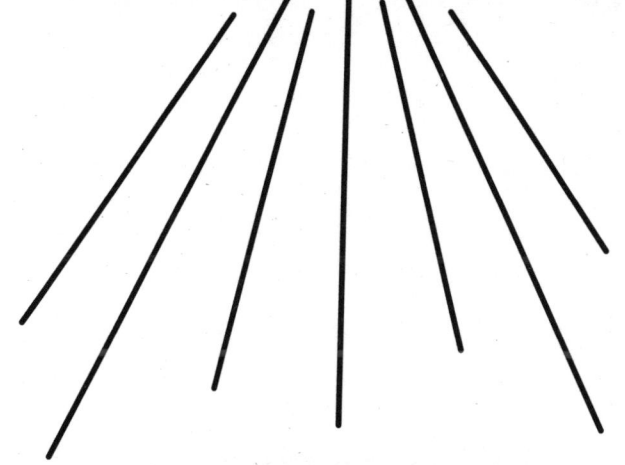

PRACTICAL STEPS
FOR MOVING FROM STUCK
TO UNSTOPPABLE

MARK FENNELL

GILL BOOKS

Gill Books
Hume Avenue
Park West
Dublin 12
www.gillbooks.ie

Gill Books is an imprint of M.H. Gill and Co.

© Mark Fennell 2024

9780717197347

Designed by Bartek Janczak
Proofread by Sally Vince
Printed and Bound in the UK using 100% Renewable Electricity at CPI Group (UK) Ltd
This book is typeset in 11.5 on 18pt, Minon Pro.

The paper used in this book comes from the wood pulp of sustainably managed forests.

All rights reserved.
No part of this publication may be copied, reproduced or transmitted in any form or by any means, without written permission of the publishers.

A CIP catalogue record for this book is available from the British Library.

5 4 3 2 1

This book is not intended as a substitute for the medical advice of a physician. The reader should consult a doctor or mental health professional if they feel it necessary.

The identities of the people in case studies in this book have been changed to protect the privacy of these individuals.

This book is dedicated to my wife Fiona, who has stood with me and cheered me on every step of the way. To my family and everyone who has supported me and my work, I say thank you.

The book is also dedicated to the reader who wants to embrace a life that is fulfilled. You deserve to have a life that makes you smile.

Contents

Introduction … 1

PART ONE
THE FOUNDATIONS FOR CHANGE … 7
1. How are you … really? … 8
2. Unlock your identity … 25
3. Your why … 45
4. Your capacity … 64
5. Your positioning … 83
6. Your time … 94

PART TWO
THE SOLUTIONS TO STUCK … 109
7. The types of stuck … 110
8. Mentally stuck: overthinking and worrying … 123
9. Emotionally stuck: trapped feeling this way … 143
10. Physically stuck: when your body lets you down … 164
11. Relationally stuck: love and sex … 192
12. Interpersonally stuck: friends and frenemies … 218
13. Historically stuck: dealing with the past … 236
14. Financially stuck: money and manifesting … 252
15. Spiritually stuck: finding true happiness … 269
16. The road to fulfilment … 287

Acknowledgements … 292
Endnotes … 294

Introduction

A few years ago, I went out with my dad to get something to eat in a bar close to the area where he grew up. Some guys were seated at the bar with a pint of the black stuff in front of them whom my dad knew from 30 years ago. When he spotted them, he called out a 'How are you?' and they all gave a grumbled reply of 'Nothing new, same old'.

It was a Thursday at 2 p.m., but to these men going to the bar was their daily routine. As we left, my dad told me how some of them had been through hard times that they'd never got over. They would sit at the bar day after day talking to whoever would listen, giving out about the government, sport and whatever was playing on the television in the corner. They all had a story to tell; each of them had had experiences that knocked them off track in life and that they struggled to cope with. Sadly, these men were stuck.

As you read this book, there are people sitting somewhere with their potential put on hold. Pain, loss, trauma, failure – a long list of reasons to be stuck.

The reason I write this book is to prevent you from missing out on your potential and to break through what might be holding you back. Don't be the man or woman at the end of the bar, or sitting anywhere for that matter, as life passes you by because you got stuck. We will all experience pain, struggle and loss. Nobody deserves that, and nobody deserves to miss out on life either. Be the person who gets so wrapped up in building a fulfilling life that you never let circumstance cut off your potential. There will be hard times, but life doesn't have to stay stuck there. This book is for those who refuse to let the station of stuck be their last stop. Stuck can be temporary or it can be permanent; the decision is yours.

This book is for anyone who has ever felt like they lost their spark. Anyone who feels trapped, bored or even a little lost. It is not just a book on how to navigate out of feeling stuck, but how to find peace, fulfilment and joy. Perhaps you are stuck trying to get healthy, hurting with a broken heart, stuck in addiction, stuck in the wrong job, lost without direction, stuck in the past, stuck with bad eating habits, emotionally stuck, mentally stuck or financially stuck. But whatever your stuck, this book is for you. I've helped thousands of people get out of feeling stuck over the last two decades and I will share with you how to do it within the covers of this book. I know how, not just because I've helped many achieve it, but because I was stuck before too, in such a way that it nearly destroyed me.

When I was in my twenties, I collapsed in the gym. I was rushed to hospital and treated for a suspected heart attack. It was the most frightened I have ever been. It opened the door to fear like I had never experienced before. Things came to a head in the form of exhaustion and burnout, leading to a complete breakdown. I was stuck being busy and from that I became stuck in chronic anxiety. The whole ordeal set in motion an internal battle as I became crippled with sleepless nights, fear and rumination. I lost 30 pounds in weight, and it got so hard to keep going that I nearly didn't make it through. However, what I discovered eventually led me to being free of the horrible anxiety and two years later I was unstuck. Something in my gut told me to hold on and hope. I rebuilt my life over the next two years step by step, brick by brick, day by day. I eventually discovered how to beat anxiety for good and what it takes to get unstuck.

Regardless of why you are stuck, there is a way out. It is possible to deal with the frustration and the pain, get unstuck and be happy.

This book is based on knowledge gained from years of helping people, the results of studies I have conducted and my lived experience. Over the years, I have discovered that no matter how badly discouraged, hurt or lost you feel, there is a way out of that place. I can testify from first-hand experience that regardless of your situation, you can find happiness, fulfilment and hope again. Even if you've been told that there is no way – there is always a way.

Here I will share the tools and strategies that I have learned. They have worked for thousands of people; they can work for you.

BECOME YOUR OWN COACH

Each chapter in this book is like a session with your own coach. I'll reveal to you the strategies and tools that will empower you to shatter your limitations and redefine what's possible.

Throughout the book, you will explore the areas that we get stuck in the most in life. I'll share profound insights into the power of your thoughts, mindset and emotions, and unlock your ability to unleash your authentic self and tap into your limitless potential.

For over two decades, I have been blessed to work with individuals from all walks of life, witnessing their incredible transformations first-hand. As you embark on this transformative journey, you'll find stories of others who have faced similar challenges. Even if their specific circumstances don't mirror yours, I invite you to discover the universal principles and apply them to your own life.

Now, let's talk about fulfilment. As the saying goes, 'give a man a fish and he will eat for a day, teach him to fish and he eats for a lifetime'.

Suppose we call fulfilment the fish. When I coach someone, they may have never even eaten a fish, never have had that sense of fulfilment. Or maybe they had it for a time, but now they don't know what it is. So, I give them the taste of the fish and then when they taste its flavour, they now get a desire to independently seek this fish, i.e. find fulfilment on their own.

I don't want to just tell you how to fix your stuck, I want to train you to be your own coach so you can get to a place where you can coach yourself.

As your own coach, you can learn to observe yourself. Instead of impulsively reacting when triggered, you'll learn to hit the pause button and ask yourself why. You'll observe your behaviours and thought patterns, with the goal of transforming them into constructive and helpful responses, gradually shifting towards a more balanced and healthy approach. It will take effort and patience, just like learning to fish, but trust me, it's worth the effort!

Throughout this journey, as you dive into the stories and insights that I will share, your self-awareness will skyrocket. You will gain greater control over your reactions and a deeper understanding of yourself. Remember, clarity is key. Understanding how and why we process things the way we do is a game-changer. Each chapter includes exercises that you can try out to address the various areas in your life where you feel stuck.

When we become stuck, it compounds over time and gets harder and harder to break free of it. It is like being submersed in a deep ocean and the further you go, the harder it is to see daylight. Uncovering your core beliefs and values is the key to unlocking your true purpose. Within each chapter, I will provide you with practical exercises, powerful strategies, and the guidance you need to break free from the chains that have held you back. Together, we'll create a roadmap to the life you've always desired – a life overflowing with joy, love, and peace. Leave behind the pain of the past and step into the brightest version of yourself. By the time you reach the end of this book, you won't just be free from stagnation; you'll be a force to be reckoned with, unstoppable in your pursuit of greatness and fulfilment.

So, buckle up and get ready for a transformative ride. Together, we'll unleash the tools and wisdom needed to break through from being stuck, so you can discover a life that is fulfilled, a life that makes you smile.

PART ONE
The foundations for change

CHAPTER 1
How are you ... really?

HOW ARE YOU AND WHAT IS IT YOU REALLY WANT IN LIFE?

One of the first questions I will ask a client is 'How are you?' After the first answer they give, which is usually short and brief, I will ask again.

'So tell me, how are you really?'

The answers I get are mixed. Some people share a lot and some very little. But I do this to evaluate their current emotional state at that time because our emotions tell us a lot. Emotions are our reactions to situations and events either present, past or in a future that we envision.

It is a question we fail to stop and ask ourselves, but, when we sit for a moment and think about how we are really feeling, we start to get insight. At the start of any journey, clarity is vital. When the captain of a ship knows the destination before setting sail, that's clarity. Sometimes we might feel like a captain of a ship that is floating in the sea with no idea of where to go or what harbour to dock in. Life is blowing us from one place to the next and our focus is on staying afloat and surviving, as opposed to having a course and plan. Our emotions are like the ship's radar, measuring how things are going. What is that emotional blip on your radar and how do you describe it? When you are anxious, sad or angry it is like a radar pinging that something is wrong.

When I discover how a person is really feeling it leads to the next question: 'What is it that has you feeling like this?'

I receive a wide range of answers. People tell me that it is because they have no direction and feel stressed, anxious or lack confidence. Sometimes it is because they want to meet someone, feel they have something to get up for in the morning, or want to know how to build a better career or start a business. The list goes on.

Sometimes the answer I get is, 'I don't know what I want, I just feel lost.' Fear and frustration can then follow as they feel adrift with no course to take.

What do you do when you don't know what you want? Or perhaps what you want is impossible for you to have? Can you still be happy if you can't have what you want?

I felt lost when all my wife and I wanted was to have children but were told it wasn't possible. We have never had kids and that feeling of being stuck and knowing that what we longed for was now deemed impossible is a tough situation to come to terms with. I'll share more later on how we coped and dealt with the news. But a great quote helped me when I was stuck and what I desired was not possible:

> **Nothing is impossible. The word itself says 'I'm Possible'.**
> **AUDREY HEPBURN**

I took from that quote that I am possible, my capacity and my potential are still there even though the road I thought I was meant to take was closed. You need to figure out a new route because you are possible, meaning your potential can never be taken away from you even in the face of impossible circumstances.

Discovering what you stand for, and what you want in life and making a plan to achieve it is the target. Maybe you know what you want and just need a plan, or perhaps you feel stuck and have lost your spark, or maybe you just want to level up in life on your journey of self-development: however you feel today, we will figure it out together. We will get you to that life you desire. Each chapter builds on the last. The book is written as if I were coaching you step by step, page by page. In this first section, we will focus on the foundation upon which everything will be built. The second section, 'Solutions to Stuck', will look at how we can apply those tools to each part of your life.

When you feel lost even though life is okay

Chloe was a young woman who seemed to have everything going well in her life. She contacted me to have a chat. She shared how she expressed gratitude for all the blessings she had, and yet, deep down, something felt off. Despite her outward appearance of happiness, she felt like there was an underlying void within her.

I asked Chloe 'How are you?' To my surprise, she lowered her head, fell silent, and then burst into heart-wrenching tears. Chloe confessed that she had been functioning in life, wearing a happy façade, but in reality, she felt no joy, no spark, and had nothing to genuinely look forward to. While she cherished her family and had good friends, something essential was missing. She longed to recapture the happiness she once felt and her enthusiasm for life. But now, she found herself trapped in a monotonous routine, unable to understand why.

'Why am I not happy?' she exclaimed.

Chloe's story is not uncommon. Many people find themselves merely existing, surviving day by day, with their heads down, without truly living. It is so important to ask yourself, how are you? It is a question we should revisit periodically; it forces us to evaluate our lives and take stock of how things truly are. Often, we become so engrossed in the hustle and bustle of life that we forget to check in with ourselves until it's too late and our unhappiness has become undeniable.

If you were sitting with me in a one-on-one session what would your honest response be if I asked you how you were and what you wanted in life? Most of us just want to be happy and feel calm. But the truth is happiness and calm should not be the goal. The goal should be things that generate happiness and calm. An emotion is a psychological and physiological response to a specific event, experience or stimulus. An emotion is a reaction to something. What is that 'something' that might generate happiness or calm for you? Because that is a better target to aim for. (But remember that true happiness and calm won't be found in money, drugs or sex.)

What we truly seek, whether we realise it or not, is a life that brings us a sense of fulfilment – a life that aligns with our deepest desires and values. Happiness can't be sustained every day, nor can feeling calm. But fulfilment comes when we are truly content with life. It is not achieved by reaching all our goals, but it is the state we obtain by knowing that, overall, life is going in the direction we want it to. It is that fulfilment that generates happiness, and the calm and positive emotions you desire. You will have stressful days and experience loss and pain. But fulfilment is not only present when you are winning. It is a heartfelt state that allows you to press on, even when you are hurt, driven by an inward spark that stops you from giving up. That spark is there because life has meaning and is valued and precious. In other words, you have something to live for.

When we pursue our hearts' desires, it creates a state of fulfilment. It is that fulfilment which harvests joy, peace and love.

After nearly two decades of assisting people on their journeys, I cannot help but notice the keys to a fulfilled life. Far too many individuals are merely going through the motions, not truly embracing life's fullness. This book is not about finding fleeting happiness; it's about achieving a profound, enduring contentment – an unshakable sense of fulfilment that permeates every aspect of your existence.

Let's be honest: it would be disheartening to reach old age and realise that you're still yearning for something you have yet to find. Living a life that falls short of its potential, a life devoid of fulfilment, is a missed opportunity of monumental proportions.

Are you in the passenger seat or the driver's seat?

In the passenger seat, you are going wherever circumstance takes you, being led as opposed to leading. In the driver's seat, it is you who decides the route for your life.

This book is not solely dedicated to helping you break free from the chains of stagnation; it's a guide to rediscovering yourself. Perhaps you've lost your way and are no longer the vibrant, happy person who once harboured dreams and aspirations. It's time to place that authentic self back in the driver's seat of your life.

OPEN THE CAGE

The last time I visited the zoo, the lion enclosure got me thinking. The lions had been in captivity their whole lives. This had been their habitat since they were cubs. They had never known freedom, never been able to walk in the wild, hunt for their dinner, or meet other wild lions. The lions were stuck, but not just stuck, they were stuck against their will. A lion doesn't get a choice of what zoo to go to when it is born, never mind if they want to be there or not. The lion's only life experience is the cage and the routine of the meals being delivered. Life for a lion moves along without too much excitement.

What is true for the lion is true for many humans too. They operate within their familiar, their comfort zone, their routine.

They don't know any different. It is the same process leading to the same result. The cage has conditioned the lion to understand that this is all there is. With a lion stuck their whole life in a cage with dinner served every day, why do we need the cage at all? Nobody has ever told the lion that all these people peering in at it are potential steaks on legs. It has never been taught to attack, hunt, or run free. It knows nothing about the African plains or the beauty of being free in the wild. To the lion, there is no more to life. The lion doesn't know its potential.

The lion has been conditioned and controlled in relation to what it can do. The same is sadly true for so many people and maybe it is true for you. You might be going through life not knowing your potential, who you could be if you weren't conditioned by fear, or perhaps if you weren't controlled by others, or if you weren't enslaved by your past. Maybe you've achieved great things and feel your best days are behind you, now what? The reason the cage exists for a lion is because of one vital thing that we too can relate to. This vital part is why the cage and boundaries get checked, why the meat is thrown in and not handed to the lion; why tranquilliser guns are left nearby. It is because of one thing. One thing that we have in common with the lion: instinct.

The invisible cage

As human beings, we can sometimes become stuck like the lion. The cage, however, is not a high fence or locked door. Maybe your cage is a job, a lack of self-belief, a habit of procrastination, a relationship, a physical challenge, a business, a controlling person, comparison, a location, a mindset, a hurt, a past event, a fear, a trauma, a limiting belief or whatever it might be.

Whatever 'cage' has you stuck, you don't have to stay there. The fear might tell you to stay with what you know, stay with your familiar. But what if freedom was waiting for you, what if healing was waiting for you, what if your purpose was waiting for you? What if a fulfilled life was waiting for you on the other side of that cage door?

What if your best days were ahead of you and not behind you?

A few years ago, I encountered a remarkable woman named Kate whose story touched me deeply. Despite her impressive accomplishments – she was a successful professional with a well-paid, high-performing job – she found herself suffering from imposter syndrome, trapped in a cycle of worst-case scenarios and debilitating anxiety. Every day was consumed by the relentless worry of 'what if this happened?' and 'what if that happened?' She became unable to sleep at night, which in turn affected her performance at work.

Kate, now in her forties, realised that this way of living couldn't continue any longer. Anxiety had taken a toll on her sleep, appetite, and relationships. Desperate for change, she reached out to me for help. When we began our sessions, I posed a question that often unveils the desires of one's heart: 'What would your dream be if fear didn't exist?' Her response was profound in its simplicity: 'To be anxiety-free and regain control over my life.'

As we embarked on this transformative journey together, little did we know that a breakthrough awaited her. After several sessions, she unexpectedly requested an emergency session. Worried that something dreadful had occurred, I made time to connect with her. To my surprise, her emergency wasn't a crisis but rather an extraordinary revelation – she had experienced a few days of freedom from anxiety, something she hadn't felt in two decades. During this anxiety-free time, she noticed the birds chirping and the scent of freshly cut grass as she walked to her car. Her sleep had improved significantly, and even the taste of food seemed richer and more vibrant. Yet, amidst this newfound calmness, she faced a different kind of uncertainty.

Her anxiety had become her familiar companion, her North Star in navigating life's challenges. It had guided her attention towards potential dangers and motivated her to take necessary actions and preventative measures. She had lived enslaved to anxiety her whole life and now it had subsided she didn't know how to feel. She felt peace of mind and body and couldn't explain it, it was so foreign to her.

Our beliefs and emotional patterns shape our perception of ourselves and our world. In her case, anxiety had become intertwined with her identity, causing her to question who am I now that I am not anxious. It was a reminder of the complexity and depth of the human psyche, and the interplay between our emotions, beliefs, and actions.

She even felt a little strange and emotional about not feeling anxious. I reassured her that such feelings were normal. Without the preoccupation of anxiety, she became more present and aware, allowing her to come alive with a heightened experience of her senses, such as smell and taste.

It's important to recognise that she had stepped outside her cage and entered a realm of freedom she had longed for. Yet, this unfamiliar territory also instilled fear because it was new and different, pushing her beyond her comfort zone. I share this to convey that apprehension is natural and acceptable, even when we get to the place we yearn to be and experience the emotions we long for. Adjustments are required as the old self adapts to the new reality. Like trying something for the first time, it may feel strange and unfamiliar. Many of us may not even be aware of the cages that confine us internally.

Gradually, she adapted to this new normal and began embracing the life she had always desired. With newfound confidence, she successfully delivered presentations without the sleepless nights that previously plagued her. The imposter syndrome became a mere whisper, as she learned to trust her gut instinct.

Try this. Think about a time in the past when you wanted to do something, but you were nervous, in two minds, maybe even afraid of doing it, yet you did it anyway and it was amazing. The feeling of achievement, that sense of winning, the joy of completion – was it worth it? Was it worth overcoming the fear, the anxiety, the knots in your tummy?

Trust your gut; it might pay off.

What is your cage?

A study published in the journal *Frontiers in Psychology* in 2017 found that people who trusted their gut feelings were more likely to experience positive emotions and less likely to experience negative emotions.[1] The participants were asked to complete a series of tasks that involved making decisions, and they were either told to rely on their gut feelings or to make the decisions based on analytical reasoning. The participants who trusted their gut feelings reported feeling more positive emotions and fewer negative emotions than those who relied on analytical reasoning.

Your gut or intuition is a part of you that can differentiate between what you want and what you need, between what is right and what is wrong. It is an intrinsic instinctual part of you driven by beliefs and values and can operate in the blink of an eye. The book *Blink* written by Malcolm Gladwell recounted many instances where people didn't always understand why they made certain choices, but upon questioning would conclude that they just trusted their gut, their intuition.

Your gut feeling is a powerful tool that can help you make better decisions. It is based on your past experiences, intuition and subconscious thoughts. It can make mistakes, but when it comes to what you desire in life it is seldom wrong.

What are the barriers holding you back? What do you need to break through? Cages come in all shapes and sizes and for each of us, the cage is different. What holds one person back may not hold another back. The reality is if you have a cage then you can deal with it and there is no shame or guilt attached.

I remember feeling so stuck and broken that my whole world fell dark. No twenty-something wants to feel like this. I decided I was going to defy statistics and break free of anxiety. Something in me said it was not over yet: I can, I will, I must get through this.

I made a decision. If ever this felt too much to bear, I would reach out for help the following day, but until then I am going to study, research and work through this. I approached it like a coach helping a client through their inner challenges. I observed myself. Many times it got too much for me and things got very dark in my life. I was slipping away at one point. I thought I'd reached rock bottom only to fall further. A small voice in me said 'Keep going'. My wife and family were incredible. It was one of the toughest battles of my life because the battlefield was my mind. After two years I eventually broke through the anxiety and fear, not by beating or resisting it, but by not fearing fear anymore. I cannot put into words how hard it was and how stuck I felt. But I trusted my instinct to hold on and keep going. That was almost 18 years ago and anxiety has never been an issue for me in all the years since. Who would have thought that anxiety and fear could be overcome? Whatever you are facing or however you are stuck start listening to your gut instinct. Let me tell you: it's not over, the best is yet to come.

My instinct saved my life and I don't know where I'd be today if I hadn't discovered it. Awakening your inner strength is just one of the things you will learn with this book. I have brought this message to thousands of people over the years and now I am bringing it to you. You were never meant to be caged. The best is yet to come for you and I want you to start believing that.

Start to listen more to your inner voice, your gut instinct, your intuition. It knows what you want even when you think you don't. Maybe it is saying something about your health, your lifestyle, a business, a career choice, a partner, a purchase, a goal, or maybe it is a gut instinct about someone or even yourself. Start to listen to this voice because sometimes our analytical mind can't see things.

> **Instinct doesn't explain why, it simply nudges you.**

WHAT IF YOU WEREN'T STUCK?

Taking the first step in getting unstuck is like a first date: there are nerves and there is the unknown, but something in you says go for it. But instead this date is with your destiny. The decisions you make today will ultimately define your future fulfilment. You can settle for what is and remain there or you can start by getting curious. What if this thing holding you back didn't exist? The first move is listening to the inner voice that is calling you to take a step: that inner voice that knows things aren't right, that inner voice that you know you can trust. That voice that told you to pick up this book and read. Is something within you telling you that things could be better?

> **Today's decisions are tomorrow's destiny.**

It has different names but they all mean the same thing. I call it your gut instinct, some call it your intuition, your inner voice. Whatever you call it, we all know it. That voice that doesn't always have an explanation but knows what the right thing to do is. Regardless of what has you stuck, getting unstuck is worth it, and more importantly, it is doable.

We may be aware the cage is there but if we never look beyond the cage we will never see what could have been. If we settle for the enclosure we are in, we close our eyes to our potential. We might as well close the cage ourselves and lock the door. If you want to remain where you are then do nothing.

Being stuck is one thing, but remaining stuck is down to you. Doing nothing achieves nothing, so why do nothing when you can do something?

THE FIRST STEP IS TO BE HONEST WITH YOURSELF

Maybe things feel out of alignment in life and you have not identified exactly what is wrong, but knowing there is something up is a good start. Your gut instinct is telling you that something needs to be looked at. It doesn't have a plan or the tools, and it doesn't even know what that destination should be. It simply is telling you that something is not right. Your gut instinct will light a spark of discovery. The beginning of getting unstuck is admitting that we are stuck, admitting there is a cage. Unlike the lion, we have the potential to step outside of whatever is holding us back and live freely. I'm not saying life will be easy, but it will certainly be easier by not allowing anyone or anything to put us in a cage again. It doesn't matter how the cage got there, what matters is whether you choose to stay there or break free from it.

Being open and honest with ourselves is crucial, and this is what Chloe, the woman I mentioned at the start of this chapter, found hard to do. She never took the time to process how she felt and felt bad admitting something was up considering her life on paper was blessed. I helped her to identify how she felt and to try and name the problem. Then I asked how she would like to feel and what might get her there. The exercise at the end of this chapter was a massive step for her because it gave her clarity, a starting point. From there we could see what she wanted to work towards.

Change your thinking, change your results

Honesty with yourself is a strength that casts light onto those dark parts of the soul that you might be used to sweeping under the rug. But what if you decided to lift that rug and face those inner negative beliefs, thoughts and emotions and rid yourself of them? Getting open and honest with yourself and declaring that the cage is about to be unlocked and you are going to step into the new, stronger, wiser, happier, fulfilled version of yourself starts with the exercise below.

EXERCISE
WHY DOES JOURNALLING WORK?

In a classic study by James W. Pennebaker, participants who wrote about their traumatic experiences for 15 minutes on four consecutive days experienced improved physical and psychological well-being. This study demonstrated the positive effects of expressive writing as a form of talking about problems. Writing for that long may not come easy, and you don't necessarily need to write for 15 minutes, but the study shows how writing helps us process things and get clarity. Here is a 60-second version to get things started.

This exercise is designed to help you discover what your instinct is trying to tell you. It is a great help when you read this book to highlight parts that resonate, take notes, and write things down when they click with you.

Sometimes we need to understand how we are feeling and why. Elaborate as much as you need with your answer to each question. Our objective at this point is to get clarity.

PART ONE: Name the problem
Q1: How are you?
A1: I feel _____ because _____
EXAMPLES:
'I feel *stuck* because *I don't have the motivation or drive to do anything.*
'I feel *lonely* because *at my age most of my friends are married and I am not.*

PART TWO: How would you like to feel?
Q2: I would like to feel more of the opposite emotion, which is _____

EXAMPLES:
'I would like to feel more of the opposite emotion, which is *happy with my life.*'
'I would like to feel more of the opposite emotion, which is *peace with my situation.*'

PART THREE: What can you do?
Q3: To feel more _____ I will _____

What is the one thing you can do today to cultivate more of the emotion you want to feel as opposed to the negative one you currently feel?

Sometimes we can generate how we want to feel with other things in our control. It won't make the negative emotions go away but it will top up the emotions we want to feel.

EXAMPLES:
'To feel more *happy*, I will *start to make time for the things that make me laugh and give me joy.*'
'To feel more *peaceful*, I will *look at my schedule and start to include the things I enjoy.*'

I often refer to this as the XYZ tool – 'I feel X because of Y, and Z might make it better.'

This exercise will help you to start processing how you feel and to find a way to remedy the situation. It is merely to get you started. It is a simple way to become self-aware.

You don't have to see the whole staircase, just take the first step.
MARTIN LUTHER KING, JR.

CHAPTER 2
Unlock your identity

WHO ARE YOU?

Feeling stuck often arises from a disconnect between who you are and who you desire to be. When your expectations and reality are not aligned, it leads to you feeling like you are not where you should be in life. You may have a vision for your life, but are you actively living it? Or do you lack a vision of what a happy, fulfilled life would look like? Sometimes you may feel that you don't deserve life to be better because, for whatever reason, you believe that you are not worthy of a good life.

When you find yourself not embodying the person you truly want to be, it can induce a sense of being trapped – a sort of identity crisis. We all go through identity changes throughout our lives. The problem arises when we aren't happy with who we are.

For instance, you may be labelled as an anxious person due to anxiety, yet you yearn to break free from this label. In my case, when the doctor told me that anxiety would probably be something I would struggle with for the rest of my life and that I would need medication, it broke my heart to think that this would be my identity. So I chose to challenge this label of 'anxious' and put all my focus and strength into becoming who I wanted to be, not governed by the limitations of a report. Rather than letting anxiety define me, I defined my identity.

Lack of confidence might be a constant struggle for you, but you don't wish for it to define you indefinitely. Perhaps you currently lack a sense of purpose, but deep down, you know that's not how you want to exist. You want to feel you have a sense of purpose and have a fulfilled life.

While you possess a current identity, you hold the power to transform yourself into the person you aspire to be. And this transformation is not some distant future possibility – it can commence right now.

Your values are foundational to your identity. When you live life according to your values, you are living as your true self. This exercise will help you to identify what those values are.

EXERCISE
TOP VALUES

From the list below pick your top five values. Start by marking the ones you find important that may potentially make the list. All values are relevant, but the key is finding what drives you. When you've marked the important ones, put a number between 1 and 5 beside them, 5 being the least important and 1 being the most important.

- **INTEGRITY:** Being honest, truthful, and having strong moral principles.
- **HONESTY:** Telling the truth, being transparent, and avoiding deception.
- **RESPECTFULNESS:** Treating others with kindness, consideration, and dignity.
- **RESPONSIBILITY:** Taking ownership of one's actions and obligations.
- **COMPASSION:** Showing empathy and concern for the well-being of others.
- **COURAGE:** Facing challenges and difficulties with bravery and determination.
- **PERSEVERANCE:** Persisting in the face of obstacles and adversity.
- **PEACE:** Feeling calm within yourself and amongst others.
- **GRATITUDE:** Appreciating and expressing thanks for what one has.
- **SELF-CONTROL:** the ability to regulate your emotions.
- **EMPATHY:** Understanding and sharing the feelings of others.
- **KINDNESS:** Performing acts of goodwill and being friendly.
- **ACCOUNTABILITY:** Holding oneself and others responsible for their actions.
- **FAIRNESS:** Treating all people and situations equitably and justly.
- **TEAMWORK:** Collaborating effectively with others to achieve common goals.
- **INDEPENDENCE:** Valuing self-reliance and autonomy.
- **GENEROSITY:** Giving to others without expecting something in return.

- **HUMILITY:** Recognising one's limitations and showing modesty.
- **ADAPTABILITY:** Being open to change and flexible in various situations.
- **AUTHENTICITY:** Being true to oneself and not pretending to be someone else.
- **FAMILY:** Prioritising the well-being and happiness of one's family.
- **COMMUNITY:** Valuing and contributing to the betterment of the local and global community.
- **ENVIRONMENTAL STEWARDSHIP:** Caring for the environment and taking steps to protect it.
- **INNOVATION:** Embracing new ideas and creative thinking.
- **HEALTH AND WELLNESS:** Prioritising physical and mental well-being.
- **EDUCATION:** Valuing continuous learning and personal growth.
- **FREEDOM:** Cherishing personal liberty and the right to make choices.
- **SPIRITUALITY:** Seeking meaning and purpose in life through faith or belief systems.
- **SUCCESS:** Striving for personal and professional achievement.
- **FINANCIAL SECURITY:** Ensuring financial stability and independence.
- **ADVENTURE:** Embracing new experiences and taking risks.
- **BALANCE:** Seeking equilibrium in various aspects of life, such as work–life balance.

LIMITING BELIEFS

Limiting beliefs are thoughts that you believe are the absolute truth and that stop you from doing certain things. They can oppose your true values.

When my body had symptoms of anxiety, my mind was racing and I was stressed and anxious all the time because I believed that anxiety would control my life. This was my limiting belief and it prevented me from pursuing my values. I didn't choose this belief – nobody chooses their limiting belief. But we derive it by circumstance, feelings, opinions and upbringing and if we say it enough, or it is said to us enough, over time we will believe it to be true.

To overcome this limiting belief there was a question I asked myself that I am going to ask you. The question is this: 'Despite how I feel and how I think, what do I want?'

My mind and body were telling me I was anxious. Yes, I definitely was in a state of anxiety, so I am not suggesting denying how you feel. The answer to 'what do I want?' was obvious. I wanted to stop feeling anxious and to enjoy life. That was my values speaking, my intrinsic desires. It wasn't even about being fulfilled, I just wanted peace within. I really valued peace and calm because I saw what life was like in their absence. I certainly did not value anxiety; who would? Yes, anxiety has its purpose in life when required, but it's not designed to be a constant emotional state. Rather than take on the limiting belief that anxiety would control my life, I focused and had faith that my current situation was not my final destination.

At the time, my values and desire for peace were but a whisper amidst tangible anxious sensations and ruminations. It was that whisper that I was going to listen to because it said 'Don't give up'.

Sadly, so many people listen to the other voice that shouts 'Give up, you won't beat this thing!' and I came very close to doing so many times. Maybe you are going through a completely different type of struggle to mine, but the rules are the same. The result you seek is possible. Eventually, I got to the place where anxiety was no longer an issue for me at all. It took time, but it all started with my identity.

The mind focuses on what it hears most often and comes to believe it to be fact. If you often hear that you are a failure, will never be happy, or are less than other people (maybe from a parent, teacher or peer), you will come to see it as a fact. But, in reality, it's just a belief that has been established over time. Who is to say it's true?

THE SEVEN STAGES OF IDENTITY

The seven stages of identity framework is a guide to how our identity can be affected by certain triggers. To break through, we need to see what could be on the other side. The seven stages of identity will help you start to build what is possible for your life. The order can change but the key thing to note is that, instead of us being reactive and living by how we have been triggered, we need to live and work from the basis that our identity is made up of our core beliefs and values.

If we live life in a reactive way it means we react to what comes at us, so how we feel and think will govern our day. This reactive mindset is easily influenced. I understand that if an emergency comes up, we have to react. But I am talking more about a daily approach. A person with a proactive mindset is someone who doesn't wait to feel a certain mood but instead, they have a long-term view of themselves and are acting with their future self in mind.

You can either be guided by how you feel, or you can be guided by who you desire to be and what you want. In the latter case, you are acting in a way that is identity-led. For example, most of us don't 'feel' like going to the gym. A person with a reactive mindset chooses to listen to these feelings and thoughts of 'I'm tired' and they stay at home. An identity-led, proactive person sees beyond their feelings and has a vision of the fitter, healthier person they are working on becoming. With that mindset they are proactive and leading themselves, so off to the gym they go. The gym is a part of the plan for fulfilling their image of who they are becoming: their identity.

You can apply an identity-led mindset to being more confident, finding fulfilment, finding love, overcoming fears, and so many facets of life that you might want to change. It is the image in our minds of who we desire to be. Are you reactive or proactive when it comes to your identity?

Look at the sequence below. We get triggered, and it fires off thoughts which influence how we feel. These feelings – emotions – influence the decisions we make and, of course, our actions follow the decisions. Over time these actions become habits and these habits cause us to establish beliefs and values – in other words, our identity:

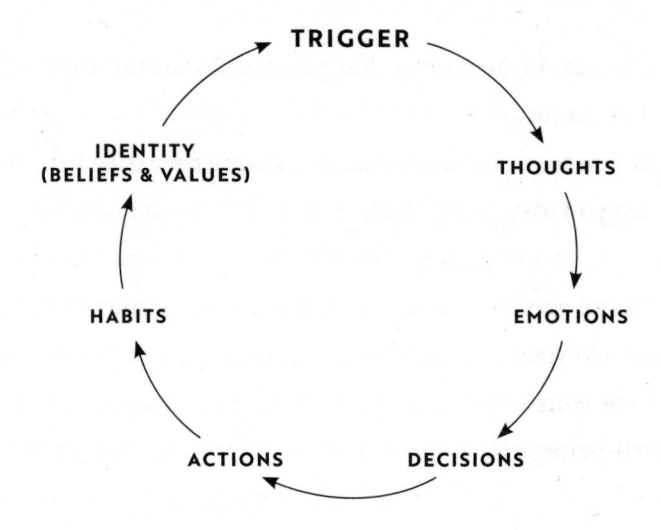

```
        TRIGGER
   ↗              ↘
IDENTITY          THOUGHTS
(BELIEFS &            ↓
 VALUES)          EMOTIONS
   ↑                  ↓
 HABITS           DECISIONS
     ↖          ↙
        ACTIONS
```

However, if we put identity at the beginning, it is now cultivated in the presence or absence of triggers. Our identity now governs who we become and we live according to our true values.

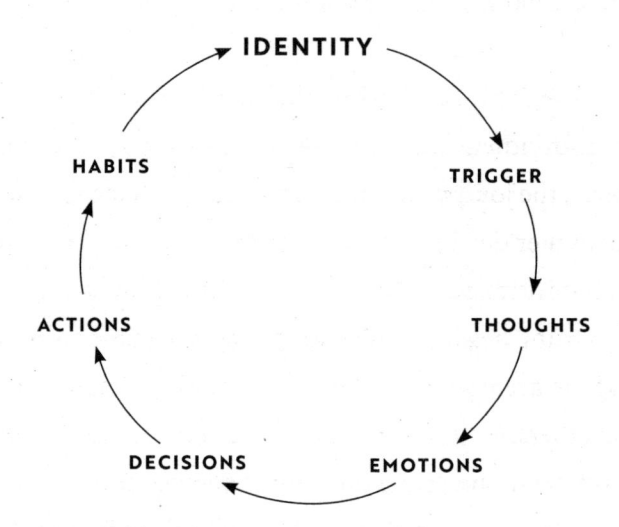

```
         IDENTITY
      ↗          ↘
   HABITS       TRIGGER
      ↑            ↓
   ACTIONS      THOUGHTS
      ↖            ↓
     DECISIONS ← EMOTIONS
```

Take a moment to reflect on your identity – who you currently are and who you aspire to become. Be honest with yourself and use these answers to paint a clear picture of your present state and your desired future.

Do you want to be someone who constantly dwells on the past? Do you want to be controlled by the opinions and actions of others? Do you want to be plagued by insecurities? Do you want to live a life filled with sadness? Do you want fear to dictate your choices? Do you want to be weighed down by depression? Do you want to be constantly anxious? Do you want to neglect your health and well-being? Do you want to play the role of a victim throughout your life? Do you want to remain stuck, unable to progress?

If your answers to the above questions are a resounding 'no', then you already have a clearer vision of who you want to be than you might think. Sometimes, in order to uncover our true desires, we need to approach it from the opposite perspective – by asking ourselves who we do *not* want to be.

Your true identity is the path to fulfilment

Every individual deserves a life of fulfilment and happiness. However, the journey of life, the choices we make and the people we encounter don't always align with that ideal.

What interferes with having a fulfilled life is replaying the past, treating negative beliefs as if they are true, becoming bitter, feeling we are not worthy, inner turmoil, hating ourselves and hating others. Getting unstuck is about finding peace for yourself even when circumstance does not encourage it.

How do you want your life to make you feel most days? The answer is within your hands and change is possible. Use the five values you identified in the previous exercise to mould how you see the future you.

Stop being hard on yourself

This book is not telling you to simply 'think positive' and that everything will work out. Nor am I telling you to ignore your feelings. It's important to remember that your feelings are valid, they do matter and it is normal to have them. You are a human being, and human beings aren't always in top form. That is okay. The key is to not let yourself be governed by bad feelings. Instead, when you feel down, let that be the moment you ask yourself: 'What's up? What's wrong? Why do I feel this way and how can I make it better for myself?'

You won't feel motivated every day, nobody does. So stop being hard on yourself when you see your friends, family or colleagues flying ahead on their gym journey or with their relationship or their new business. Nobody stays motivated all the time because motivation is a state of mind and an emotional state that will peak and fall. It's okay if some days, you don't want to pursue your goal or you simply want to chill out. Sometimes you need a day off. Time off is needed, just don't stay there because it can get comfortable. Let's be honest.

It is okay not to be okay every day.
It is okay to have bad days.
It is okay not to feel motivated all the time.
It is okay to want to quit.
It is okay not to always be positive.
It is okay to want to rant.
It is okay to be frustrated.
It is okay to be afraid.

Your response is your responsibility
In the space between being triggered and responding, there is a moment of choice. It is a place where you have control. You must decide what your response to a trigger will be. You can respond with how you feel in the moment or you can respond with your true identity, the person you truly want to be that is true to you.

> **Between stimulus and response is a space. In that space is our power to choose our response. In our response lies our growth and our freedom.**

Eimear was treated terribly by her boss in a job she loved. She felt stuck because she had to continue to work there in order to build up her qualifications and experience but struggled daily with his narcissistic ways. She would talk about what she hated all the time. The negative mindset became her normal, as she went to work thinking over and over about the horrible day she was about to have. When she started working with me, I got her to take a step back and observe the situation as an onlooker, and I asked her: 'What will you learn from all this?'

She identified several things that she was going to learn from her tough situation: professional skills like how to handle difficult people, being able to identify manipulation and building resilience were just a few. Slowly, this new insight led to change, and she became adept at not letting her boss's words impact her emotions because she could now see the bigger picture. She had a new identity in the forefront of her mind that was built on her top values like perseverance, accountability and success. Understanding that this hardship would make her stronger, she was able to get to a point where she could see every bad situation her boss created as an opportunity to observe and grow.

> **A person can take away your joy only if you give them permission to.**

If you let negative people into your head, they can take control of how you feel. However, having a clear identity alongside a power statement can act as a wall to keep their destructive arrows out.

CREATE YOUR POWER STATEMENT

The key to achieving change is not motivation, but finding your reason for wanting change in the first place (your 'why'). Your why needs to compel you so that it will propel you. You need to really care about your reason why, not just have it as a nice sentiment. Your why needs to keep you moving forward even when you don't feel like it. We will discuss this in more depth in the next chapter.

When I was struggling with anxiety, finding my why changed everything. I pushed forward, never giving up with the hope that one day I would conquer anxiety. I decided on three things to make up my why:

1. Giving up was not an option, I would keep going no matter what, for me, my wife and my family.
2. If I could overcome anxiety, I could help so many people.
3. Life without anxiety would mean peace. Peace became my top value. I would do whatever I could to generate calm and peace.

That was my why and for me it made me press on even when I was in the throes of anxiety. I also came up with my own power statement:

I CAN

I WILL

I MUST

I can

Saying 'I can overcome anxiety' was a reminder to myself. I didn't know if I could do it, but I knew I could keep trying. I failed lots, but when I had even one per cent of the progress I wanted, I acknowledged it. Sometimes I would take one step forward and two steps back. Whatever barriers you need to break through, start saying 'I can'. When you fail or lose, keep hope and say 'I can do this'. These simple words can have a profound effect when we have the passion to keep going. I used to visualise myself speaking on stage to people about my journey to overcoming anxiety. For me, saying 'I can' is a commitment to not giving up and holding onto hope. Don't give up no matter what.

I will

'I will' was the faith that I could get to a peaceful state of mind, even if it was only for a short time at first. I reckoned if anxiety could come into my life, then it could also be removed. Of course, normal anxiety is natural, but the levels I had were chronic. If you are stuck because of a lack of confidence, memories or an absence of joy, start saying 'I will find a way'. Believe that you will figure out how to experience the emotions and mental state you so desire, like being happy, calm or confident. 'I will live according to who I desire to be.'

I must

The 'I must' part of the mantra related to my family and the people I wanted to help. I must get there for them. It was not about me, it was about them. 'I must get through this so that I can help others get through whatever their challenge is.' Create your statement or use mine. But let it be so compelling that it simmers within you constantly. Without thinking, say whatever your statement might be. Maybe it is a scripture, a proverb or a quote. But whatever it is it must have meaning in it: otherwise, it's just a sentence. It needs to be your mission statement, your new belief and value all wrapped into one. It might be short and sweet like 'I got this'. Or something like 'I'll be okay'. Whatever it is, just feel it and believe it. For it to be most effective it needs to be from your heart.

EXERCISE
YOUR POWER STATEMENT

Discover your own power statement with these prompts:
- Who am I when I am at my best? Describe yourself in three words.

- How do I want to feel most days? Write down three emotions.
- What new habits can I do that achieve the previous two answers frequently?

These questions might give you a guide to a statement that is not just words, but that you feel and mean with conviction. It's like your mission statement.

CONFIDENCE

It's only right we talk about confidence because to make change you need to have just enough of it to say 'I can do this'. The word confidence means to have faith in or rely on something. Self-confidence is your ability to rely on yourself.

Confidence is built slowly and consistently by discovering that you can rely on yourself to survive what you fear.

Just look at your past and the things you thought you'd never get through, but you did. Use those memories to cultivate your new, confident identity. It is not that you are confident that you have all the answers to whatever life throws at you. It is the knowing that whatever comes your way, you won't give up or lose hope. That is a mindset of confidence in and of itself. The more you rely on yourself, confidence responds.

If you want to feel more confident around others ask yourself, 'What small change could I make?' One of my clients suggested this: 'I could be the first to say hello and shake their hand and then I could have an icebreaker question all ready to go.'

Through repetition, their confidence rose in social settings because they were proving to themselves that they could trust themselves and not be awkward.

Alison had a very poor self-image. She would never be in a swimsuit even though she used to love swimming. We came up with the bitesize technique of starting by just buying a swimsuit. Then Alison tried it on at home. After that, she went to the local gym and after her exercise, she went to the swimming pool changing rooms, put on the swimsuit, had a shower, got dressed and went home. She didn't go to the swimming pool. After doing this a few times, one day she saw women leaving the changing room to go for a swim. She said to herself, 'I'm going swimming,' and she walked straight out and into the pool. Her confidence in her appearance went up tenfold because she took action, albeit in tiny steps. She now loves swimming again and does aqua aerobics and even sunrise swims. She got unstuck and overcame her fear.

I run programmes specifically around weight and body image, and it is all about baby steps taken consistently, and having a clear goal of who you desire to be and how you desire to look. It's identity-driven. But whatever your confidence level, and regardless of what area it is lacking in, it is crucial to keep your future self at the forefront of your mind and to have a plan to get there. Confidence starts within.

If you struggle with confidence and feel stuck because of it, start taking the tiniest of steps. Confidence will grow over time, so give yourself all the time you need and go at a pace that is not too challenging.

> **It is not about being fearless, it is about being brave.**

It's not about being fearless, it's about having a little more courage than fear in order to act. Fear won't be gone, but building our inner Braveheart will give us enough courage to face our difficulties. Who do you want to be? Afraid or brave? In that very moment when you feel the fear, you make a choice about how to feel: brave or afraid?

SMART GOALS

To beat procrastination, build confidence, have a healthier lifestyle, achieve a healthy weight or start a project or business, SMART goals are a great tool. They allow you to cultivate change at a healthy pace. The idea is to break down your plan to achieve what you want to achieve into realistic increments. It is better to spend some time planning a job than just launching into it. Create a plan using the acronym SMART. I explain it below and share an example of someone who used it to lose weight.

S: SPECIFIC

An exact goal with details, as opposed to a vague general one.
EXAMPLE: 'I want to lose weight' is vague. A more specific goal is 'I need to lose 10 pounds'.

M: MEASURED

What gets measured gets managed. This way you can gauge progress.

EXAMPLE: In order to lose 30 pounds in a healthy way I need to lose 1 pound a week.

A: ACHIEVABLE

A goal that is possible and not overwhelming.
EXAMPLE: It is possible and healthy to lose one pound a week.

R: REALISTIC/RELATABLE

A goal for you that is realistic but also relatable, doing it for you and nobody else.
EXAMPLE: I am losing weight for myself and for the right reasons, in a healthy way.

T: TIMED

Having a time on the goal keeps you accountable and on time.
EXAMPLE: I check in periodically to see progress and by a certain date I will have lost 30 pounds.

A simple place to start is to break down what you need to do into bitesize pieces. Remind yourself of your why, which we will discuss in detail in chapter 3. Be clear: does it align with your values as I focus on my future self (identity)? Press through the pain barrier: it is uncomfortable to grow and change, but it is worth it when we get to the other side. Act despite what you think or how you feel, and you will develop great resilience and discipline.

IDENTITY

Who we desire to be needs to be the driver behind the wheel. Listen to your heart and become self-aware. Look at the sequence and allow your true identity to decide who you are in the very moment you are triggered or derailed. The moment your old self tries to act on its old habits, you revert to your old identity. Get into the character of the person you desire to be. Ask yourself, 'What do I need to do in response to this trigger? Who do I need to be at this time of stress?'

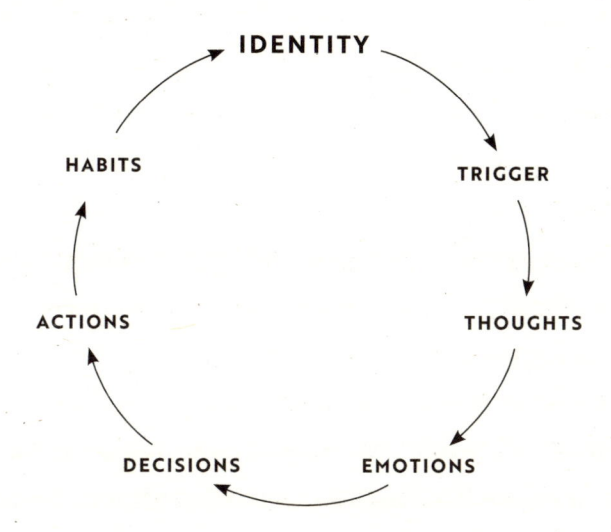

IDENTITY → TRIGGER → THOUGHTS → EMOTIONS → DECISIONS → ACTIONS → HABITS → IDENTITY

When something triggers you, instead of letting it dominate your thoughts, you call into action who you are. Your identity says you are a victor, a person of resilience, a survivor, a thriver, a person who has been knocked down but keeps getting back up. When the thoughts try to automatically go back to the old you, your heart will speak and get your thoughts in line. Refer to your power statement at this time. Your emotions will try to fall back to the negative emotions like they used to, but you are not your thoughts, and you are not your emotions. They are secondary. Your new identity is primary. Fear, anxiety, depression, low self-esteem or pain – you feel them, but they won't define you. You acknowledge them, you process them, but then you focus.

Your sequence now starts and ends with who you are and who you are becoming. All the decisions you now make will be in line with who you are and your values. The habits you create must encourage the person you are. The new beliefs that we will establish will confirm who you are. You are not made to be stuck; you are made to live life.

Wherever you are from and whatever past you have, let today be the day you decide to pursue a life that is true to yourself and your identity, not what people say or what society expects. Start living a life that practises gratitude for the little wins, stresses less over what's not important and helps you to respect yourself; a life that leans into love and controls your ego. A life that holds onto hope despite fear. Life is a gift, it is a blessing. The purpose of life is to really live it. The purpose of life is to feel alive. In the next chapters, we'll outline how to find that life you so desire, and also deserve.

You are not stuck anymore, you are becoming unstoppable.

CHAPTER 3
Your why

WCPT

In the following chapters, we will explore a tool I refer to as WCPT. It is the foundational stage of getting unstuck. Rather than add things into your life with the hope they will cultivate change, a wiser method (and one that I have seen clients succeed with) is to take the approach of looking at your life as it is and paving the way for the next chapter. It is just like when a gardener prepares the soil before they plant a tree. If the ground is not right, the tree may not flourish.

WCPT stands for Why, Capacity, Positioning and Time.

WHY: Your why is the spark that ignites a drive within you, it is your intrinsic motivation.

CAPACITY: Your capacity refers to your mindset and how to cultivate a growth mindset.

POSITIONING: Your positioning refers to the people you are surrounded by, and how to discover the right people.

TIME: Your time is an asset, and we will look at how to make it work better for you.

Let's start by looking at your why.

LACK OF MOTIVATION

The hardest thing to do is to take action towards change when you don't feel motivated. The lack of motivation makes the thoughts of change appear like a lot of work. In fact, it's why people stop doing things they had every intention of doing. In order to get you unstuck, you are going to need motivation. This is not just feeling energised, it is much deeper than that. So, we need to make sure your 'why' is right. It is the deep reason you have for wanting to make things better for yourself.

My anxiety stemmed from an incident in my twenties when I collapsed in the gym. One minute I was training and the next I started to see dots in front of my eyes. Suddenly, I felt faint and then collapsed, clutching my chest. I was rushed to the hospital and treated for a suspected heart attack. We later discovered that the pain in my chest was an injury that spiked at the same time as I fainted. They kept me in hospital and concluded that the cause of my collapse was exhaustion.

My collapse led to me developing chronic anxiety and post-traumatic stress. My spark was extinguished as fear entered and anxiety consumed me. I felt broken. Daily anxiety took away all my happiness and peace. How was I ever going to start making things better? I wanted to be well, but felt so lost and so afraid of my own mind. I felt hypersensitive to my body and surroundings, and experienced overthinking in social settings about having an anxiety attack or collapsing again. I just wanted to stay at home and my motivation to do anything was gone. But even when I was at home, there was no respite from this torture. I couldn't relax, I was in a state of fear due to the trauma. I felt like anxiety could pounce at any moment and I was on high alert. The truth is, whatever your stuck is, it becomes a mindset.

Maybe you can relate. Maybe you have been knocked and your spark is gone. You have no motivation or drive to put effort into the things that might be of help. For me, I had been so focused on building my business that I neglected balance. Anxiety was a tsunami that drowned out motivation and drive. It was like the joy in life was taken away and I started to question everything. *What's the point? What's my purpose? Why is this happening to me?* I felt so broken and so vulnerable. Have you ever felt like everyone else had a happy life but you? I was slipping away. My weight was falling and so too was my morale; things got very tough.

How you feel is not always a guide to what to do

When we wait to 'feel like' doing something, we are letting our emotions take charge of what we do. I discovered that this is not a good habit to forge. For example, you fall in love and in the early stages you are filled with all the butterflies and excitement of being in love. But those butterflies eventually have their wings clipped when the realities of life hit, and you may not feel head-over-heels over in love with your partner every single day, especially when they annoy you. So, does this mean if you don't 'feel' in love, it is time to break up? No, of course not. Feelings are valid, but commitment is a choice that we make even when we don't feel it. Emotions are a reaction, not a map of what to do next.

When illuminated, our spark will light the way for us and it won't rely on our emotions. It's a motivation that shows up in spite of how we feel. A spark is a value within, coupled with a belief.

It is the why behind the what. It is that drive within that pushes you on. Unfortunately, life sometimes throws water on that spark, and maybe you need to get yours back.

Emotions and motivation are transient, meaning they are changeable. Motivation will come and go. Don't wait to feel ready to start, simply trust your gut instinct and listen to that voice calling you to make change and start this journey. You won't have motivation, but you just need to want change badly enough.

> **Getting into the right mentality does not necessarily mean waiting for the right emotionality.**

The comfort zone

We often choose what's easy and familiar, but this can lead to settling for less. Many stay in jobs they don't like out of fear of change, or simply because they don't know that there are other options.

For most, it comes down to having a fixed mindset. The fear is too much to change anything, because what if it doesn't work out? A lot of people are stuck because nobody presented them with an alternative. For me, I had to start to try and imagine that anxiety is fixable and that I could be happy again. Doctors and online blogs all said that it was for life and that there was no way through it without medication or therapy. I am not against either. I had to give myself the hope that there was a way. I knew I needed to have the right mindset to take actions not governed by how I felt. I knew I needed to take control. Even though I didn't know if anxiety could be controlled, I was willing to double down and try. You may not even know what your gut instinct is saying or what it wants. Start by asking yourself, 'What do I not want to feel, what is the opposite emotion?' That is a guide, so let's make a plan to get there.

> **Frame your life, or your life will frame you.**

VICTOR OR VICTIM?

There are two ways of being in life. You can be a victim in life or a victor. The difference is mindset. Mindset is what steers our lives into who we become. My podcast was inspired by the aim of sharing with people the importance of the right mindset. You can think in one of two ways – life either happens to you or it happens for you; you decide how you see it.

I was struck by the story of a man named Nick Vujicic, born in Australia with tetra-amelia syndrome, and so he has no arms or legs. His life was filled with challenges. He endured bullying, depression and loneliness, and he battled thoughts of suicide for years. He felt like a victim of his circumstances and believed that he would never live a fulfilling life due to his disabilities.

However, Nick underwent a profound transformation. He realised that he could not change his physical condition, but he could change his mindset and attitude towards life. He found the strength to embrace his uniqueness and develop a deep sense of self-worth.

Nick's life changed when he became a Christian. With newfound determination, he started speaking publicly about his experiences and how he overcame the challenges in his life.

Nick travelled extensively as a motivational speaker, touching the lives of millions with his powerful message of hope and resilience. There was no bolt of lightning; it all began with a decision he made to be a victor, not a victim. You have that same decision to make.

The victim mentality: fixed mindset

Victim mentality is the mindset of a person who believes that life happens to them. They blame their problems on the world, the government, their upbringing, their school, their teachers, their past, their ex, or the risks they took that didn't work out. Everything that had a negative effect on them is the reason they are unhappy now. Of course, bad events and horrible people will impact life, but you decide if you will allow them to influence your future. Your past can only influence how you feel today with your consent.

Perhaps you have undergone serious trauma – but don't let it ruin your life. Get professional help. The key is to get the help rather than let it influence how you feel now and in your future. You will see as we go through the book how to change your mindset. You may have been a victim of an event or person, and of course that merits help and healing. But don't see yourself as a victim forever. A person may be a victim for the time the horrible thing happened but they are not a victim indefinitely. It may be a part of your past, but it doesn't have to be a part of your identity.

The victor mentality: growth mindset

The victor takes the position that whatever happens to them, they will survive it and be okay. It is a hopeful mindset focused on the faith that they will be okay regardless of adversity. They know that there will be pain and suffering in life, but they focus on how they will feel after the pain passes. They don't give up. They are motivated by the good things in life that they value.

The key difference is that the victim focuses on the trials and heartbreaks and the victor focuses on the other side of the trials and heartbreaks. The victor spends time working on solutions, learning and growing through challenges. The victim is more interested in proving that things can't change. The victor works on creating the way they will feel in the future. The victim spends their energy justifying their present frustrations. A victor believes they will be victorious in the end, not conquering other people, but overcoming their inner fears, anxieties and hurts as a person. They will come out the other side, and they take responsibility for their future. We are all given opportunities to be victims of life, but that just closes the cage on our future.

If you want a different result, you have to change the process

See yourself as responsible for your future by having a victor mentality. The process can be your routine, lifestyle, career, outlook or mindset. Whatever part of the process is lacking will have a domino effect on your life. Consider the process that has resulted in your current state; give yourself the chance to get unstuck and start now.

PROCRASTINATION

When we want to change something, we sometimes fall foul of procrastination. Here are three reasons why people procrastinate.

1. People procrastinate because they want to avoid how the change will make them feel. They avoid the action because of the emotion. The emotion in question might be the anxiety of taking a chance on changing career or starting a business, the stress of having to learn something new or the suffering of saying no to food you love.
2. People procrastinate because they feel it is too much to do or the risk is too great. Feeling overwhelmed stops us, as well as thoughts of failure.
3. People procrastinate because they are waiting for things to be perfect to start. Things will never be perfect, so waiting does nothing but prolong the start.

The truth about procrastination is this: if you want to grow, build anything of value and find fulfilment, it will be scary, you won't always like how it feels and there will never be a perfect time.

DO IT FOR OTHERS, NOT JUST FOR YOU

The world can be a selfish place at times, but ironically, we humans are social creatures, meaning we need people. We are more geared towards having a community than being isolated. We aren't built to think only about ourselves, yet the world is filled with selfishness.

Pat struggled with alcohol his whole life. His marriage was failing and divorce was now the topic of conversation during his moments of sobriety. He was a functional alcoholic running his own business. Pat hit rock bottom when he had an affair, and was now sleeping in his car and drinking so much that one night he was hospitalised. He wanted to end it all.

He spent time in hospital for depression and was on suicide watch. It was there that a nurse told him about me. Through a few sessions, I could see he was struggling with demons from his past. Then in one session, he had a light-bulb moment. Every time we chatted, it was always about him. So I said, 'Imagine if you helped people get over what you're going through?'

I did this deliberately because what I have seen from experience is that we as people work a lot better when we have others in mind. The key is to identify who that might be. It wasn't his wife, although he loved her; it was a sense of purposeful work that lit him up. I discovered that this was actually his motivation years earlier for getting into finance: he loved helping people achieve their dreams like securing a mortgage or buying their dream car.

He hadn't lost his purpose, but he had lost sight of it along the way. Helping people is what gave him the intrinsic why that he had been searching for. He now had a purpose. Pat went on to work with alcoholics; he sat with them and did the detoxing with them. He never drank again. Despite losing his business, he was able to save his marriage and has helped many people overcome addiction and ultimately find their purpose again.

The power of Pat's why highlights the significance of intrinsic motivation. It is a force that can push us beyond our perceived limits and drive us to take extraordinary actions when faced with seemingly insurmountable challenges. Pat's will to help people gave him such purpose that it was the guiding force that allowed him to prevail and beat alcoholism.

Understanding our motivations and having a compelling why is so often linked with our purpose. Everyone who is stuck wants to be unstuck, but *why* do you want to get unstuck? For me, there was something in me telling me to do it not just for myself, but for my family. And what if one day I could help others do the same? My why was focused on others, and that's how I began to see things differently. I was doing it for them, not just for me.

Whatever the answer, most people will agree that we just do not like how being stuck makes us feel. Why we want to change is a major element in getting unstuck.

Below are two lists: extrinsic factors that motivate people's actions for a short time, but rarely lead to any internal substance or fulfilment; and intrinsic motivation that comes from our true selves, aligning with our values. Intrinsic motivation is longer lasting and generally results in what really matters to us as humans.

Extrinsic factors can be likened to when you get a gift, and unwrapping it makes you feel delighted with life, but the joy soon subsides. It is like winning at something only to realise that you have to keep winning to sustain this satisfaction.

Intrinsic factors are much deeper and are things money can't buy. They are the real pearls that make life come alive. They are like the moment you find purpose in something you do or the love that motivates you to commit your whole life to another human being. They are powerful motivational factors. These are what you need to tap into.

You can probably think of a time that you were so focused and committed to getting something or doing something it took up 100 per cent of your focus – like a final exam that you stayed up all night to study for. Or a time you worked so hard you forgot to eat. Or when you discovered a purpose that changed your life, like Pat did. These moments are driven by deep intrinsic motivations.

Can you remember a time when you were so focused that it propelled you forward?

Extrinsic factors motivate but only give short-term fulfilment and satisfaction in life

- Money
- Praise
- Competition
- Threat of punishment
- Fame
- Image
- Possessions
- Notoriety
- Position
- Power
- Grades
- Approval

Intrinsic factors motivate and lead to long-term fulfilment and satisfaction in life

- Seeking fulfilment
- Achievement
- Happiness
- Love
- Purpose
- Contentment
- Excitement
- Peace
- Gratitude
- Safety
- Security
- Freedom

For example, the person who works late can be motivated in one of two ways. They work late to gain approval and praise, or they work late because they get enormous fulfilment from their job. Fulfilment became my why. For me, nothing else fulfils me like helping someone. My objective to be free of anxiety was motivated by that very same reason, it wasn't about me anymore.

When you let others be the focus or your why, watch what it does for you. It is like what a parent will do for their baby. Or the people who march for injustices. Firemen and women who risk their lives to save another. Or the many good Samaritans who do what they do for others with no self-interest.

TERI AND THE DESIGNER BAG

Teri grew up with very little money. She left school at 16 and went straight to work as a cashier. One day while on the job, she encountered a rich woman with a designer handbag. This led her to start thinking about role models and how amazing it would be to be comfortable enough that you could treat yourself to such a beautiful bag. She couldn't stop thinking about this wealthy woman and decided that she wanted to be like her. She wasn't interested in the money, but the freedom money would give her. She came from a very poor background and money was a constant stress.

What Teri was actually doing was forming in her mind a new identity that was not hindered by poverty. It wasn't about being rich, it was about being free from the fear of lack of money. Her motivation was security and freedom.

Teri worked very hard and upskilled her abilities. Ten years later, she landed a job in sales that she'd always wanted and went to celebrate by buying something nice. She saw a designer handbag worth over a thousand euro. She thought of how far she had come and realised that she was now the successful woman she had worked so hard to be. She had never bought anything like this before, but could not stop thinking about the bag because for her it represented so much. She bought it.

It may seem strange, but it wasn't about the bag. She told me: 'It's just like a trophy for me. I don't care if anybody sees it, it makes me feel I've achieved something. I've never felt like I was worthy of such a thing, I always felt like a second-class citizen because of my background. But now I value myself enough to buy myself an amazing treat because I am no less than anyone else.'

For Teri, her motivation was completely internal, the bag represented a sense of achievement and fulfilment from her hard work. It wasn't about showing off or bragging. It was a personal symbol of success.

The bag was not her why. It was just the external evidence of her new identity, a mark of personal achievement. Be led by your intrinsic factors in your pursuit of the life you desire. And celebrate the wins along the way however you see fit, even if it means buying a treat for yourself. Teri broke out of her limiting belief that she couldn't have nice things. The bag was proof for her.

HAVE A SAFE SPACE TO TALK

On your journey of getting unstuck, it helps if you have someone you can talk to, and they can also act as an accountability partner. It could be a trusted friend, confidant or coach. You're going to need encouragement on those tough days. The only way a person can grow is when they talk about how they feel and embark on the task of changing and fixing it. If you take on the belief that you must be positive all the time, then you will bottle up emotions, and this is not always healthy to do. How we feel is valid and needs to be recognised and talked about in the right space. The key to growth is to be open and honest with yourself and your mentor if you have one. A lot of people don't have someone to confide in, and that's where journalling comes in. Journalling is a great way to write down how you feel and why you feel it and make sense of inner struggles. So become open and honest and, whether it's a person or a journal, get talking or writing. In my case, the notes in my phone became an unofficial journal, and it was there that I would turn when I needed to remind myself of things that would encourage me.

FIND YOUR WHY

Discovering your why will enable you to reach heights you never thought you could get to. It will help you put the work in, make the changes and strengthen you on days you feel like quitting or giving up.

Studies of athletes have shown that strong intrinsic motivation is associated with higher levels of persistence and willingness to face challenges. When individuals have a genuine interest in achieving a goal for inward satisfaction, setbacks are viewed as opportunities for growth, and they are more likely to persevere. We can set realistic objectives for ourselves, but most importantly we must make sure we are motivated for the right reason. The right, healthy inner motivation is key. Motivation means a reason or reasons for acting or behaving in a particular way. I want to help you establish the true factors that drive you. When you discover these drivers, you now have an inward motivation that will keep you focused at times when emotionally you may not feel motivated or driven.

The difference between motivation and your why is this. Motivation is an emotional state we can experience that can come and go, but your why is a constant inner value. Maybe your why is your kids, a loved one or being able to help others. Maybe it's to conquer the impossible or to defy statistics. Maybe it's because they said you can't and you will show them you can.

Whatever it is, let's figure it out.

Pursue what you value

An internal motivation is not a feeling but a value. It is that intrinsic value that you are in pursuit of that will keep you going. The word motivation is derived from 'motive'. A motive is a reason someone does something. What is your motive?

To get unstuck, don't try to become something you are not by being motivated by external factors. For example, trying to get a better job because you'll get more money is not going to keep you satisfied in the long term. When I ask clients what is the why that drives them, most don't know, they just do what they do with little or no thought. It's no wonder so many people feel stuck: their only motivation in life is to clock in and clock out. A lot of us are more driven by being productive as opposed to being fulfilled. Find your inner motivation and you begin to find purpose.

How to identify your why

Here is a simple tool to identify your past why, your past spark, so we can get you fired up again today.

EXERCISE ────────────────────────────
SUCCESS CIRCLES

STEP ONE: Grab a pen and paper. Draw three circles beside each other, large enough to be able to write in each of them.
STEP TWO: Label them as C1, C2, and C3.

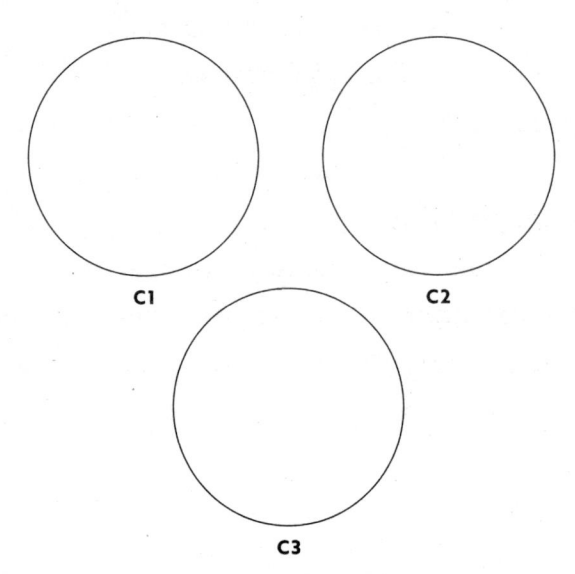

C1   C2

C3

STEP THREE: In C1, write down three achievements that really meant something to you. They may be personal, academic or professional – things that you were thrilled to have done. There is no wrong answer.

STEP FOUR: In C2, describe how you felt when working on those achievements. Revisit how your mindset was and how you felt emotionally. What was driving you to get it? What was your why, your motivation, your inner spark? Did you work later than ever before, was it all you could think about, and why was that? What did it mean to you? What did the fact that you wanted this so much say about you? What made you keep going?

STEP FIVE: Write in C3 about the challenges you faced and overcame. What was hard about it? Was there anything that nearly made you stop or quit? What was the hardest thing about it? What resistance did you experience within? You may also find this circle will help you add to C2.

From this simple exercise, I want you to take a moment and pause. Think about how you felt when the challenges came your way and you persevered. What was on your mind when you woke up each day and went to sleep? How did you feel? How focused were you?

I want you to tap into the mindset you had at that time so that you have a sense of what you need to feel as you progress, in order to achieve that new goal of tapping into your true self. The best athletes are not always the fastest or the strongest, instead they are the ones who best deal with pain, can adapt to change and can endure hardship. Hard times make you discover what you are made of. If it doesn't break you, it will make you.

How to know if it's a good wine

Your why is like your fuel. It is what you draw on when you struggle and when you are growing. Good or bad, it is the constant thing that spurs us on. Your why is something you need to keep at the forefront of your mind. It will help you decide what is important and what isn't; whether your journey is one of personal growth, career growth or business building. You need your why to keep you on track.

Your why is like a grape. A vintner knows the quality of the wine they produce is based off the quality of the juice inside their grapes. But the truth is, nobody knows until the grape gets squeezed. Until pressure is applied, we don't know what lies inside. When pressure is put on a person, then you see what they are made of.

The same is true for relationships, friendships and family. You can see how strong loyalty is when pressure is applied. The strength of any relationship is not truly known until it is tested. Only then can you see the quality of the relationship. This is why knowing what you stand for and why you stand for it really does matter. Many people try to grow and change their lives, but many fail. One of the main reasons is that they have a weak why. Your why needs to have your future interests at heart.

EXERCISE ─────────────────────────────────
FIVE-MINUTE JOURNALLING

Here are some prompts for finding your why. Answer what you can – if you don't have an answer to all of the below yet, don't worry. You will by the end of the book.

Keep the previous exercise in mind as you answer these questions in your journal:

What is your intrinsic motivator for getting unstuck?

What is the reason you want to be unstuck?

What is pushing you?

What do you want?

Why do you want it?

Who do you want to be?

Reaching your potential is not luck, it is a series of right decisions.

CHAPTER 4

Your capacity

THE POWER OF A THOUGHT

This chapter is about your capacity. This refers to your mind's ability to comprehend that change is possible. We will explore how you can achieve the capacity to level up your life regardless of past pain or limiting self-beliefs and truly believe in yourself. You will learn to increase your internal capacity to make way for your full potential. In other words, making space for a bigger vision for your life.

Many people are stuck because they cannot imagine there is anything better or that there is a way out of their situation. This is why we must increase your capacity to believe that it is possible. This starts with your mindset.

One of the most powerful lessons I ever learned was about the power of our thoughts. But the funny thing is, I wasn't choosing to make this discovery nor did I awake one morning asking myself 'I wonder how powerful thoughts are?' In school I never recall being taught about thoughts or about our thinking, and the word mindset was never mentioned. But later in life I would discover something that I think every school should teach. Self-belief, mindset, confidence, happiness, peace, courage and fulfilment are all as a result of our thinking.

I realised as I got neck deep in psychology, personal growth and biographies that mindset is either a powerful resource or a destructive one. I'm going to share with you what I believe is one of the greatest lessons you could ever learn. The power of your thoughts.

Please don't lick the furniture

Whether we choose to or not we are thinking of something all the time, consciously and subconsciously. This supercomputer we all harness between our ears called the brain is pretty amazing. Here is a funny example of what I mean when I say the brain is amazing. You are sitting somewhere right now. Your brain knows what the colour of things are and how to describe them. But believe it or not, it also knows what something would feel like if you licked it. Have a look at an object in the room. You probably have an idea of what it would feel like if you licked it. Your brain can create an estimation of the sensation based off your memory of touching similar things with your fingers. It is funny I know, but amazing at the same time. Now stop thinking of licking the carpet and keep reading.

Our mind can describe things visually, but it also knows how things feel to touch. Our mind can even create what it thinks things will feel like even if we have no history to refer to or draw from. This is actually in part how our mindset works. We have a trigger, for example 'I'm hungry', and then respond with a thought such as 'What will I have for breakfast?' In a very fast instant, and I mean very fast, your brain presents an option, along with an image, a projected memory of the taste and smell, and from that you decide if you want that or something else. Am I in the 'mood' for that experience and how will that experience make me feel? We present a question and our brain rushes to find a solution with images and memories. Our brain is just like Google search, we search for an answer or try to make a choice on something, and it brings to the forefront images, words, descriptions and even emotions that are connected to how the choice may make us feel.

It will even bring the memory of an emotional state back to us. For example, have you ever passed by a place you used to go when you were younger and the nostalgia brings back all the happy memories? The place has emotional associations that you love. The same is true when we hear of a place or person with whom we associate negative memories and emotions. Just their name may trigger memories, images and emotions all of a sudden, making you feel like you used to feel back when you were around them. Thoughts have power. So how can we make them work for us as opposed to against us? How can we control our thinking to steer clear of negative emotions and focus more on positive ones? It isn't that easy because your mind has its own agenda and that's what we will start with.

The truth about thoughts

The fact is, you don't have control of your thoughts all the time. Your brain is constantly analysing your life for threats and has an inbuilt survival instinct. You would love to be able to forget the times in the past that brought you pain and suffering. But as you and I know, memories can be triggered out of nowhere.

I want to show you how you can use this supercomputer to your advantage, helping you to get out of that rut and towards the life you deserve to have, living life on your terms.

MINDSET: THE GAME CHANGER

When I say capacity, I am referring to your mind's capacity to comprehend that change is possible. In order to change our minds, we have to be open to new ways of thinking. Our mind also has what we call inner narratives. These are the words and visualisations you have about yourself on a frequent basis, comments about how you see yourself as a person and life in general. They are like statements you believe and even live by. You establish these narratives because you believe them due to repetition: they are part of your beliefs. I have heard many negative narratives over the years in my coaching practice. Some of the most common ones are:

- 'I'm not enough.'
- 'Everyone is better than me.'
- 'I didn't have the same opportunities, so I'll never be as happy as those who did.'
- 'Good has happened so that means I'm due some bad.'
- 'I'm a failure.'
- 'I'll always be like this.'
- 'I'm unlovable.'
- 'I'm ugly.'
- 'I'm fat.'
- 'I'm stuck.'
- 'I'm a disappointment.'

Whatever it is you say to yourself, you not only think it, but you feel it. The inner narrative creates an emotional feeling which results in your state of mind. When this narrative is played in your mind on a regular basis it becomes a belief because, due to repetition, it sticks. It then becomes an automatic thought. Which means you repeat it to yourself whenever it is triggered. But what if this belief is not true? It is then a culprit that you must identify and delete, because these beliefs are most likely limiting you; hence they are called limiting beliefs.

> **Whether you think you can, or you think you can't – you're right.**
> **HENRY FORD**

The mind learns what it hears the most

Maybe your boss says you need to do a better job on a task. As you walk out of the office you think, 'I'm a failure.' The event triggered this automatic response. It is automatic because you have felt like this since your school years when that teacher said you were no good. You've looked at your siblings and your close friends and you feel you're not as clever as the others. You always struggled to fit in. This automatic thinking pattern surfaces. It lies in wait for you, ready to be triggered. You tried fighting it a few times, but it has now become a belief about yourself. When the boss hits on this old familiar trigger, it all comes flooding back. Your best isn't good enough, you're never enough, it has always been like that. This is ANT: Automatic Negative Thinking. It happens when you are so used to thinking about yourself like this and it has been repeated so much in your life that it only takes a simple statement or event to trigger off this thought process. The one that says: 'I'm not enough.'

Discover your ANT

What is your automatic negative thinking pattern? What is the narrative that shows up for you?

When does it commonly show up? What tends to trigger you?

Here's an example: you go on a date and they don't follow up, just like the last date didn't, and the narrative in your head says 'I'm just not pretty enough' or 'there's something wrong with me'. You watch your phone, checking it randomly throughout the day. You start to criticise yourself. You ask yourself, 'Why did I say that, why did I do that, did I play too hard to get? Or did I throw myself at him too much?' Round and round you go ruminating. The thoughts of 'I'm no good at dates' has now turned into 'it's because I am ugly'. You blame your body, your hair, your clothes. You delete the dating apps and give up on dating, only to start feeling even more sadness at the prospect that you might be alone forever.

Years ago, whenever I was invited out, my ANT was 'what if I have an anxiety attack at dinner in front of everyone?' and 'what if I never get over anxiety?' We all have our own versions of 'what if' that trigger us.

How you feel has a massive bearing on the decisions you make, which subsequently control the action you take. Our automatic responses repeat over the years and become a subconscious habit. As they are repeated, these thoughts and reactions reinforce our beliefs.

When the thoughts, images and narratives are consistent over time, they establish our mindset. The event has passed, but we relive it, and this reinforces our conclusion of how we see ourselves. It becomes a sequence that is sitting there ready to fire off. Your mind becomes 'set' in a certain pattern. So, when you want to change your life, mindset is fundamental. To move on from the state or mindset we are stuck in, in we must change how we think. This thinking change increases our capacity to develop more of a growth mindset that can see beyond the current negative position we want to be free of.

We can apply the seven stages of identity to the above dating scenario. (Of course, you can apply them to whatever your situation and triggers are.)

You go on a date and you really like them. You say goodnight and don't get any follow up over the following days.

TRIGGER: They never followed up, just like my last date three months ago.
↓
THOUGHTS: What's wrong with me? Am I ugly? Am I annoying?
↓
EMOTIONS: You feel sad, frustrated with yourself as you look into the mirror, you feel despair.
↓
DECISION: You decide to give up dating, as the rejection is too painful.

↓

ACTIONS: Apps get deleted, you withdraw from your social scene and going out.

↓

HABITS: This withdrawing becomes a habit and how you have always dealt with hurt.

↓

IDENTITY: You see yourself as a lonely old woman feeling depressed. This triggers more thoughts and emotions, and you get stuck thinking nobody wants you. The cycle continues.

Disarm the trigger

The key is to break or intervene in the sequence. If you can form a negative inner limiting belief through repetition, then you can do the same with a new, healthier belief. When triggered, you have a chance to change those negative thinking habits or the self-sabotaging traits. Intervention in the sequence involves formulating a better served perspective and reaction to the memory or event when triggered. Basically, you are disarming the trigger. You can take the power and impact out of negative beliefs by creating a new healthier response. This is all part of getting out of that rut. A thought has power to build us up or break us down (see chapter 8).

THOUGHTS AND EMOTIONS: THE POWER COUPLE

A thought becomes a belief through repetition, but emotions have a part to play as well. When you are triggered, you react with thoughts. What you believe about the thought evokes an emotional response. You hear a particular song on the radio that reminds you of a holiday years ago and it brings back happy memories and emotions. The song triggers a memory, images and an emotional response: that's why it is significant.

The same thing can happen for negative situations. This could include the first time a parent shouted at you, the time a teacher scolded you in front of the class, your first heartbreak or maybe even something more traumatic. When we have a negative experience, our emotional reaction causes that memory to stick around. It shocks us, so it sticks. Our mind recognises that this particular moment in life got a very big emotional reaction, so it must be important and it must be remembered. Our thoughts and emotional reactions are a power couple. Control or change one and you can influence the other.

Your level of emotional reaction to a thought tells the brain it is important to you. Emotions are a part of being human, but they also can be a hindrance. This is why we should not make emotionally fuelled decisions as we can overreact to things when our emotions are elevated. If we want to change an ANT, we must change our thoughts and our emotional reaction. It's easier said than done, but possible.

Thought patterns are hardwired into our brains

A trigger that generates automatic negative thoughts coupled with an emotional response can be changed through repetition. This change is actually evident under a microscope. This ability of the brain to reorganise its structure is called neuroplasticity. It is the brain's remarkable capacity to adapt and grow throughout our lives.

The evidence

One particularly inspiring study led by Dr Michael Merzenich and his colleagues at the University of California, San Francisco, showed that this incredible potential lies within each of us.[2]

In this study, conducted with adult monkeys as participants, the researchers focused on the brain's ability to transform itself. They skilfully trained the monkeys to perform a specific task. The areas of the brain associated with this task exhibited profound changes in both structure and function. The brain cells responsible for processing the task became more proficient, and the corresponding brain maps expanded in size. The monkeys' capacity to comprehend the task increased.

Similar studies involving humans have underscored the existence of neuroplasticity (the ability of the brain to form and reorganise connections). Investigations into individuals acquiring musical skills or mastering a new language have revealed tangible transformations in the brain's structure. These changes include increased volume of grey matter and enhanced connectivity between brain regions relevant to the particular skill. Capacity changes to accomplish a task.

The brain has remarkable potential to reorganise itself in response to learning, experience, and the dynamic interplay with our environment. This proves that a mindset can tap into the capacity for growth and change, meaning everyone who desires to put the work in can embark on transformative journeys of personal development. Basically, changing your mindset is like plastic surgery of brain. Let me use an example.

THE TEXT MESSAGE THAT CHANGED EVERYTHING

Róisín came to see me in the aftermath of her marriage breakdown. One day she read a message that popped up on her husband's phone. It was signed with an affectionate 'babe'. Over dinner, she casually asked about his plans for the next day, only to hear about a business trip to Cork to meet a male client. But her gut sensed something amiss. She discreetly investigated, uncovering photos on WhatsApp that exposed the truth – her husband was having an affair.

The revelation shattered their marriage, leading to a painful divorce. When Róisín sought my guidance, the dust had settled, but she felt trapped, unable to see beyond the ruins. Her once-beloved partner had abandoned her for a younger woman, leaving her to grapple with rejection, embarrassment, anger, sadness and frustration. In her vulnerable state, she even started questioning her own worth. Did he leave because she had become old and unattractive? In her mind, she twisted the narrative, blaming herself for not being fun enough, pretty enough or sexually enticing enough. These thoughts spun endlessly, tormenting her wounded heart.

As a coach, a big part of what I do is help people to get clarity. It transpired that her trigger for all this inward self-attacking had originated a few years earlier when her ex-husband told their mutual friends over dinner, as a kind of joke, that she wasn't fun anymore. It triggered in her a feeling that maybe the relationship breakdown was partly her fault. She felt that she prioritised the kids too much and did not pay enough attention to her husband.

What I have observed over the years is that the victim will often self-examine and start to blame themselves. We try to make sense of the other people's actions towards us, and we start over-examining the past like detectives. Sadly this overthinking will sometimes lead a person down a path of despair and self-blame. Always start by getting clarity and making sense of things first, assessing what's happening and why. We broke down Róisín's situation with the following tool. Whatever your struggle is, the same tool will be useful, so simply replace the answers with your own. (There is an exercise at the end of the chapter explaining more.) For Róisín, it looked something like this.

TRIGGER: My ex says it's my fault, he blames me, this triggers self-examination, fear, heartbreak.
↓
THOUGHTS: Was I a bad wife? What did I do to deserve this? Where did I go wrong? Why?
↓
EMOTIONS: Depression/anger/feeling judged/feeling rejected/sadness/shock.
↓

DECISIONS: I'll never be happy now that I am divorced, who wants a single mum of three?
↓
ACTIONS: I lose all focus in life, can't enjoy life, I pull back and withdraw from everyone, feeling broken.
↓
IDENTITY BELIEF: I am stuck, broken, unlovable, damaged goods, jealous of those who are happy.

What emotional goggles do you wear most days?

You can see above how shock followed by sadness, anger, frustration and feeling rejected are powerful emotions and an understandable reaction. These emotions don't just come and go, they stick around and fuel our thoughts. Thoughts feed emotions and vice versa.

I liken emotions to goggles. When we feel a certain way, we see things a certain way. If, for example, we are angry about what somebody said to us at work and then something completely separate happens at home, we might react angrily at home because we are already wearing our angry goggles.

Anxiety works the same way. We see the world through fearful eyes, always fearing the worst. Similarly, feeling that you are no good, you might go about your day acting according to how you feel. Whatever your emotional state, it influences how you interpret conversations and interactions.

Ask yourself: What negative emotion do you feel most commonly? How does it hinder you? What would be a different narrative for creating a better emotional response? In other words, is there another way you could look at the situation that would lead you to feel differently? For example, would taking a breath before you react help?

Repetition

The most important chemical process necessary to rewiring your brain is repetition. The brain is designed to store the messages that are repeated most often. When we have something that we cannot stop turning over in our heads it is because it is apparent to our mind this thought is very important, due to the emotional and sometimes physical reaction it got from us. The more emotion in our reaction to a trigger or event, the harder it is to shake a series of thoughts.

The solution

If a belief can be established through repetition, then a new, healthier belief can be established in the same way. What we need is to identify the way a belief gets established, and this gives us our blueprint for establishing new, healthier beliefs. Having an open mind to new ideas is key. Here is a simplified way to create and cultivate a new belief.

Holding onto a limiting belief is like putting your potential in a box.

Our mindset is like a car radio. It tunes into automatic thought patterns unless we force it to change. We can't avoid all triggers, but we can decide what we do with that trigger using the thoughts that follow.

You can't fix a problem with the same mindset that created it.

To fix a problem we sometimes need to change our mindset, otherwise we keep getting the same results. For Róisín, the game changer was when I asked her to share with me moments from her past when she felt lovable. These are historical moments in her life that cannot be changed in spite of how she feels now. She recalled times her son hugged her, a friend who spoke about her in Róisín's wedding-day speech, her parents at her graduation and a Christmas gift that she received when she was younger. A list of moments and memories that made her feel loved.

But it was more than just feeling loved; I highlighted to her these are also times she was appreciated, respected, desired, wanted and needed. These were facts that her limiting belief tried to discredit and take away from her. We made a plan: the next negative trigger would be the cue for her to focus on those positive facts.

Every time Róisín was triggered, she would respond with: 'I am loved, I am enough, I am a good person and I have facts to prove it.' She would also visualise those positive memories to enhance the emotional response. It wasn't just words, she truly felt those words and memories.

The key to this was these statements also had a memory of facts and evidence to back them up which I got her to write down for herself. Over time and by repetition these happy memories and statements became reinforced, and she began to get unstuck within herself. Look at each of the seven stages of state and create strategies to integrate change. For Róisín, working on thoughts and emotions was key, as well as how she saw herself (identity).

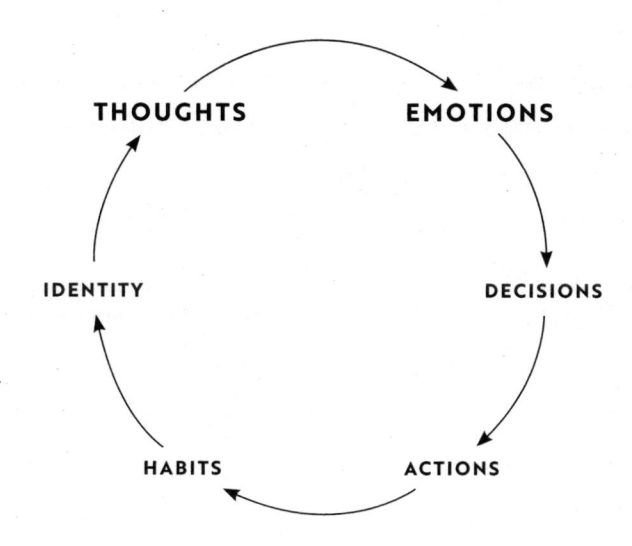

```
        THOUGHTS  →  EMOTIONS
           ↑            ↓
        IDENTITY     DECISIONS
           ↑            ↓
         HABITS  ←   ACTIONS
```

Your story may be different to Róisín's, but you can still apply the same technique and prove the opposite of that limiting belief. I bet I can prove you are loved and there is a purpose for you being here right now. We can't change the past but we can change how we see it and how we respond to it.

Emotions can be indirectly influenced through our thinking and what we focus on. Amazingly, when we start to intervene and deliberately create this positive mindset, we become more aware of and susceptible to seeing positive opportunities. As I mentioned, our mind starts looking to prove that these positive statements are true in our present. Repetition and emotional reaction is key to making it stick. You give yourself the best chance when you are convinced of the real facts, and not the false narrative.

DO AFFIRMATIONS WORK?

Speaking positive words about yourself is good. But to really see change, the words need to mean something to you; they need to have images associated with them and emotions to follow them. There needs to be a mental image or a memory of you embodying what the positive words are saying. Saying 'I am lovable' is futile unless you present yourself with threads of proof in the form of facts from your past or present.

Or if you have no past memory of this new, more constructive way to feel, you need to imagine and visualise yourself feeling and being lovable in your future. If you are to believe that you are loved, it starts by not just saying it but being open to believing it and feeling it. It doesn't come easily to speak and believe these positive affirmations, especially when your inner beliefs are so strong and resistant to them. This is why repetition and consistency are key. Like every seed, it will eventually bring fruit to bear, but it takes time, it takes work, it takes discipline. You can also establish a role model for yourself as a focal point of what you will be like if you struggle to imagine a happier, more confident you.

> **It is not the size of your brain or your wallet that defines success, it is the size of your thinking.**

A thought has the power to make your day or ruin the moment

A dream remains a dream unless we develop the capacity to believe that it is possible to achieve. Everyone you meet has a dream or goal they'd love to reach. But studies have shown that less than three per cent of people have ever written their goals down.[3] This is partly because they don't believe they can do it, or they fear trying it. This is why we must get our mindset to have the capacity to believe that change is possible, and this is why I start there with people. Negative thinking is a narrative that will keep us in the same position. Maybe your mindset needs a little plasticity in its thinking.

EXERCISE
FIVE-MINUTE JOURNALLING

Using what we have discussed in this chapter, identify the event or triggers that cause you to believe negative statements about yourself. Then look back and identify memories that clearly prove the contrary to those triggers so that you can start to build a new mindset and beliefs that serve you well. If you feel, for example, that you are single because you are not enough, let me share an example using that belief.

Write out:

What triggers you commonly?
EXAMPLE: *When someone asks me when I am settling down, it reminds me that I am still single and most of my friends are settled down with kids. Or if I see that someone younger than me is married, it triggers frustration in me and I beat myself up for not having found someone yet. It leads me to feel inadequate, different, and it results in a sense of failure.*

What limiting belief do you respond with?
EXAMPLE: *I am not enough, I am less than others because I can't find someone to love me.*

Now identify memories that prove an alternate healthier belief.
EXAMPLE: *There is no way to define what is enough or why I am not enough. I have people who do love me. I can only do my best in trying to find a partner but the fact I haven't found someone yet doesn't mean that I won't ever.*

Create a new response when triggered.
EXAMPLE: *My future happiness is decided by me not those who reject me. To feel enough is my decision to make and is not defined by my relationship status. It is better to be single and happy than to settle for married and sad. I will find someone, so I will just do all I can do and be patient.*

Be repetitive.
EXAMPLE: *Every morning I start the day with something uplifting to get my mindset in a good place, like gratitude and focusing on who I am. Instead of scrolling on my phone, which results in me comparing myself to others, I put on music. There is more to me than my relationship status. I am enough and I am blessed. I choose to believe that when it's meant to be, it will be.*

To change our mindset takes consistency and repetition. The mind believes what it hears the most often.

Consistency always trumps occasional brilliance.

CHAPTER 5
Your positioning

GROUNDHOG DAY

Just as plants rely on sunlight and shade, you too are influenced by where you are positioned in the world – what you see and hear. You absorb what you surround yourself with. If you regularly spend time with negative people, you either become like them or develop a dislike for their negativity, leading to negative emotions either way. The people you spend time with greatly influence your decisions and perspectives.

Positioning means putting yourself in a position that is subject to an influence. It is not necessarily just a physical location you go to; it can also be what you listen to, watch or the people with whom you engage. In the 1993 movie *Groundhog Day*, Bill Murray's character is forced to relive the same day no matter what he does. 'Groundhog Day' is a term we use when we feel that life is just on repeat. Perhaps you are living for the weekend to escape your job, but then the weekend comes and it too leaves you still stuck as you face into a new week. Where is the escape?

DEREK'S STORY OF STUCK

Derek came to me for help. He was stuck in a job where none of his colleagues enjoyed their work. Customer conversations always began with a discussion of the weather. Colleagues had the same repetitive conversations during lunch breaks, leaving Derek feeling trapped and unstimulated. Although it was a 9-to-5 job with no real stresses, Derek felt like he was a robot going through life. He had once felt excited by the challenge of working up the ranks in his career, but now he had plateaued and thought, now what? Each day was the same: get up, work, lunch, work, dinner, put the kids to bed, TV and then bed. Groundhog Day, as he called it.

One day, he stumbled upon a question I posed on Instagram: 'If you didn't have to work for money what would you work at?'

It made Derek think. What was his dream? This thought kept coming to mind as he observed his current Groundhog Day routine. He realised he had the capacity to change and this inspired him to start to search. Then, one weekend while visiting a local market, he realised it lacked a coffee stand. Derek was passionate about coffee. The more he thought about it, the more he imagined having his own stand.

When he shared this idea in work, he was met with scepticism and negativity, with his colleagues listing all of the reasons it was a silly idea. They pointed out the potential challenges of being self-employed, but they missed the greater cost – regret.

Regret outweighs financial loss. Taking chances, even if they don't succeed, offers invaluable lessons and opportunities for personal inner growth. When asked, those near the end of their lives regret not taking more chances. The fact that Derek noticed the question about careers showed that he had started to search for more. Surrounding ourselves with supportive people is one aspect of positioning that is crucial. His colleagues lacked a growth mindset, they were fixed in a mindset that self-employment was dangerous and risky. Their negativity affected his confidence, so he never took the chance until he positioned himself around like-minded people when he joined my online coaching group Tribe.

Position yourself with like-minded individuals who celebrate your aspirations. Derek found support through my coaching and connecting with other entrepreneurs in the group. When you position yourself with the right people, things started to happen. If you can't find them locally, consider joining a community like Tribe, where growth-minded individuals from around the world gather to discover and achieve the life they desire, whether it is through personal or professional goals, or both.

Derek eventually left his job completely to set up a coffee shop. A year later, Brian, one of his old colleagues, came up to buy a coffee. Brian said two things that struck Derek. The first was that the company had closed its Irish branch and everyone was made redundant. The second was even more shocking. Brian said that he wished he had the courage to make the leap and do something like Derek had done. If Derek had stayed in the old company he would have lost his job anyway and the security he thought he'd had wasn't so secure after all. Derek offered Brian a job and he now works with Derek.

Sometimes we don't take a leap of faith because we are fearful that it might not work out ... but what if it does?

Be mindful of what you absorb, as it influences your outlook. Surround yourself with those who uplift and encourage you. Don't let fear or financial security prevent you from pursuing your dreams.

Regret is a higher cost than any failure
Remember, the right people can make a significant difference in your journey to success but so can the wrong people. Be aware of who you allow to influence you. Positioning is not just the people in your life. It also includes the things you watch and listen to. Anything that causes you to think needs to be monitored. Are you positioning yourself in the right place, absorbing what is leading towards your desires, or away from them? Influences can be:

- Parents
- Siblings
- Extended family
- Friends
- Teachers
- Bosses
- Colleagues
- Movies
- Books
- Culture
- Religion
- Social media
- Podcasts
- News and mainstream media

BELIEFS AND VALUES

Beliefs and values are the guiding principles that shape our thoughts, actions and decisions. They start to be formed at an early age from what we hear and observe. They become so embedded in our psyche that we see them as facts to live by, so much so that they form our identity (as we discussed in chapter 2). Our beliefs about ourselves, whether healthy or limiting, define who we become. To put it simply, if we believe we are not enough we will make decisions, actions and habits based on that belief. In the same way, if we believe we have potential to be fulfilled we decide and take actions based on that belief. Your beliefs about yourself will mould who you become and the potential you will reach in life. Beliefs are self-fulfilling, whether we realise it or not. They are the pillars upon which we build our lives and pursue our dreams. They provide a moral compass, ignite passion, and create a sense of purpose that propels us forward, even when faced with adversity. Our beliefs and values can define how we navigate adversity and they ultimately decide how we will be after it has passed.

Beliefs are deeply ingrained convictions that we hold about the world and ourselves. They are the lens through which we perceive reality and interpret experiences. Beliefs can be empowering or limiting, depending on their nature. Cultivate a belief that getting unstuck is achievable for you.

Values, on the other hand, are the fundamental principles that guide our behaviour and shape our character. My value was focusing on how me being unstuck would help other people's lives. Values define what we consider important and provide a framework for making choices. Beliefs and values inspire us and are the driving forces behind progress and transformation.

A vital belief is self-belief

In 1976, psychologists Ellen J. Langer and Judith Rodin conducted a study focusing on the effect of self-belief on the physical and mental well-being of residents in a nursing home.[4] Residents were put into two groups. The control group received standard care, while the experimental group participated in a programme designed to encourage them to take control of their lives and adopt a positive mindset. This included encouragement, motivation and statements that fuelled self-belief. The programme involved empowering the residents to make choices, encouraging them to engage in activities that challenged their physical and mental abilities, and fostering an environment of support.

The results were remarkable. The residents in the experimental group, who were exposed to the belief that they still had control over their lives and the ability to improve their circumstances, demonstrated significant improvements in various measures of physical and psychological well-being. They reported feeling happier, more energetic and more satisfied with their lives compared to the control group.

This study highlights the transformative power of positive beliefs and values in shaping individuals' perceptions of their capabilities and their overall well-being. By instilling empowering beliefs and values, such as resilience and optimism, individuals can experience real evident improvements in their mental, emotional, and physical health.

This research shows the potential for beliefs and values to influence not only our behaviour but also our perspective on experiences and our overall quality of life. It emphasises the importance of cultivating inspiring beliefs and values that promote personal fulfilment, resilience, and a positive outlook. Beliefs and values can lead to transformative and uplifting outcomes for individuals, families and groups.

Be aware of what you tune into because it will have an influence on your beliefs and values. Position yourself with the right people and the right influences as much as you can in order to increase your self-awareness and aid your capacity to grow.

Pigeons and eagles

If you want to feel more fulfilled or confident or overcome negative emotions, or you want to level up your career, position yourself with the right people. Sharing your space with the wrong people can cause you to lose heart. Not everybody wants to see you do well, sadly, and not everybody may be able to comprehend your goals. This is why we need the right people to support and encourage us.

I remember something my dad once told me: 'Imagine you are a bird, ready to fly, but you have never flown before. You know you can do it but you just don't know how high you can fly. So you ask a pigeon to show you how high it can fly. You would then take off and only fly as high as the pigeon flies because to them, that's the highest you can fly. However, if you asked an eagle how high it can fly, you would end up soaring far higher than the pigeons.'

What he was saying to me was not to let what others do be my limit. A lot of people live like pigeons because it's all they know, they do what the other pigeons do because that's what seems right. Going with the crowd is safe and not taking chances is easy, but this is conditioned thinking. 'Keep the head down,' as they say. They are conditioned to think like a pigeon because they only hang out with pigeons.

But eagles soar above the pigeons, they see lots more of the world from heights a pigeon could not even comprehend. Eagles have experiences and knowledge that pigeons aren't even aware of. If you want to reach your full potential don't get limited in your thinking by asking those who don't understand or appreciate what you are pursuing. You have to look to the people who are soaring higher than you. These are the people you can learn from and who can help you to discover your potential. It's not that you are better than anyone, it is just you are not limited by other people's fears or beliefs. There is a saying that my wife frequently quotes when having to do a part of the business that we don't enjoy. I love it:

> **If you are prepared to do what most people won't, you'll have what most people can't.**

Whether you are looking for personal or professional growth, this applies. It can be hard when you are sacrificing your weekend to work on your business while everyone else is out partying. It can be hard not to order dessert because you are trying to be healthier even though the rest of the table are delving into apple tart. It is easy to go with the crowd, but is that who you are or what you want? Position yourself around the right influences and your capacity will grow out of what you believe you can achieve. If you spend all your time with people who eat apple tart, then chances are you will too, even if you don't want to. To be who we desire to be means we need to spend time around those that encourage us, not the opposite. I am not saying to cut people off, I am just saying, make sure you have the right balance of those that support your journey. Being an eagle doesn't make you better than anyone: it does, however, make you a better you.

Fears and stress can come in the form of 'what if' statements, which we might be all too familiar with.
- What if it doesn't work out?
- What if it is all too much?
- What if I fail?
- What if I don't know how?
- What if I get stuck again?

This is where having a support system is key. You need people who love you and are there for you so that on those 'what if' days when fear tries to set you back, you can call on your cheerleaders to back you up. It is not about how fast we grow; it's about getting consistent with whatever pace suits us. The worst thing to do is nothing.

Do nothing and nothing changes.

Start small, get a feel for things and see where it takes you. You might just end up soaring higher than you ever thought you could go.

EXERCISE
TAKE A MINUTE
Here is a good little challenge. Take a minute to write down the names of three people outside your immediate family who you

consider to have knowledge that may help you. Now go and reach out to them. Perhaps meet with them or have a call. Keep it casual and ask for their advice by simply explaining that you want their thoughts on possible next steps for you. They could be a life coach, business owner, entrepreneur, relationship coach, pastor, teacher, trainer, career coach or anyone you know who could help. Talking helps us to process problems and find solutions.

Take action and reach out to them. The key is making a move and getting things moving to prepare the way. Having a confidant or mentor is a great asset to growth. You would be surprised how helpful people can be.

EXERCISE
TAKE FIVE MINUTES

In this next exercise we are going to examine the things we do and consume that influence us. Take five minutes and write under the three headings provided.

ADD IN something into your life that you feel will influence you in a way that positions you towards what you are seeking. This could be joining a membership group, a podcast you'll subscribe to, a time to read the right books or time on a weekly basis to chat to someone (perhaps a coach). It should be something that will influence you in the way that you want to be influenced.

REPLACE something that you feel is not serving your positioning well. An example could be replacing some of your lunchtime with reading, walking, studying or researching. Or it could be choosing to not go drinking as much as you usually do and replace alcohol with a soft drink. Replace something with an alternative that serves you better.

REMOVE from your life that which is not helping you or serving you well. Maybe it's negativity or a toxic environment like a friendship that is filled with gossip. That thing you do that you know is no good for you has to go.

ADD IN	REPLACE	REMOVE
Example: More time to move, walk or exercise	*Endless scrolling on phone with researching instead*	*TV watching one night of the week*

But what if I fail? ... But what if you don't?

CHAPTER 6
Your time

CHASING YOUR TAIL

We have covered finding your why, capacity and positioning, but a major pitfall for a lot of people who want a better life is a lack of time to build it. This pressure, and feeling like you are always chasing your tail, leaves you lethargic and simply overwhelmed at the idea of starting something new in an already overwhelmed schedule. This stress not only affects our capacity, but it also influences our performance, which causes us to feel either overwhelmed or out of sync. This positions us away from being in a positive, productive state. There are many causes of stress, but one of the biggest is having too much to do and not enough time to do it in.

Time. We don't know how much we have, it's always counting down, and you can't make any more of it. When it comes to time, think about it like money. Are you spending it wisely or wasting it?

> **Time is the most valuable thing
> a person can spend.**
> **THEOPHRASTUS**

Whenever I start helping a client, I must deal with any stress or feeling of being overwhelmed that they are experiencing caused by how we spend our time. This is a key factor that many people tend to neglect when they want to make a change. You might add in new things to an already busy schedule only to get overwhelmed, which leads to you reverting to the old habits and feeling like you failed. When you want to make changes there is a process that works. It is just like gardening. You must get the soil right first before planting anything new. So many attempts at change fail due to people trying too much too quickly. It is a mistake to try and adopt a new mindset while still trapped in a highly stressful lifestyle.

> **It is not that you are doing too much,
> you are doing too little of the things
> you love.**

Rather than fixating on what you need to add to improve things, take a moment to identify what needs to be removed from your life; a factor that hampers our growth and acts as an obstacle not only mentally and emotionally, but also physically. This powerful element is stress. A stressed mind is not fertile ground for new ideas or a new mindset.

One of my clients once said: 'If I wasn't so stressed, I'd enjoy life much more.' In this case the person just didn't want to feel stressed anymore. It is not what they wanted to add into their lives to feel better that mattered: instead, simply subtracting stress would lead to a happier life. I discovered that the less stressed I felt had an impact on the levels of anxiety I would feel. It sounds obvious, but when I looked at my stress levels I was indirectly dealing with my anxious state.

Decompress of stress

Feeling overwhelmed and stressed is like being submerged at the bottom of the sea. You can't really see the light and all you are aware of is the pressure. When diving, a diver will slowly resurface using time and speed monitoring, otherwise they can get oxygen bubbles in the blood which can lead to decompression sickness (the bends), which can be life-threatening. One of the first things I do when coaching is very similar to helping a diver to resurface. Helping you to get your spark back requires removing the pressure of stress and feeling overwhelmed so that you aren't feeling stuck at the bottom of the sea, but moving at a pace that suits you.

What is stress?

Stress can be an emotional and physical state we find ourselves in when we are faced with a threat, under pressure, fearful, angry, frustrated, overwhelmed or nervous. Our brain responds to threats with stress but unfortunately it doesn't know the difference between something stressful that happened in the past, present or future or stress that is real or imaginary.

Stress can also arise when we are just busy all the time with no time to get proper rest and actually switch off. This prolonged sense of being 'switched on' can result in mental and emotional burnout, as well as physical issues such as irritable bowel syndrome, headaches, high blood pressure and high cholesterol, to name but a few.

Avengers assemble

Your body, which is in sync with your thoughts, releases adrenaline to prepare you for the perceived threat, whether it is a mental image or physical reality. Your fight or flight response, which is controlled by the amygdala, located at the base of your brain, kicks in. It tells your adrenal glands to pump adrenaline into your blood stream, along with the stress hormone cortisol. Your heart rate elevates, blood rushes to the muscles to prepare for the imminent threat. Your brain also draws blood away from the parts of your body that aren't as helpful when under threat. This is why we lose our appetite when stressed, as the digestive system is not too helpful when fighting a lion or an internal stressor. The body is now ready for what you have perceived as a threat and you feel it physically. Thoughts lead you to an emotional and physical state of alert and being on edge. It is just like calling in the Avengers to suit up.

Types of stressors

PHYSICAL THREAT

A person on the street confronts you because they feel you took their parking spot. They are shouting and waving their hands in your face. After the threat passes, the adrenaline lingers for a little, but then the body goes back to business as usual. Nothing a cup of tea won't fix.

Minor and major things can be a physical threat, especially something that could threaten your life. For me, the anxiety that my heart was going to stop was a major stressor. Even though it was not a reality, any sensation in my chest would trigger the fear and cause me great stress. A physical threat is something that could lead to physical danger or harm.

PERCEIVED THREAT

You hear in the canteen that a possible cutback of staff is coming and you think to yourself, *oh no, I hope they don't fire me*. Worry sets in: you can't eat, you can't sleep. Your body has the same response even though there is no physical threat.

The threat of feeling that you have no purpose, no spark and no joy can give you a similar physical reaction in your body. This is why beliefs and values are so vitally important when it comes to perceived threats. If something you value is threatened, like your job, relationship, sense of purpose or future plans, you can react with stress towards it. Stress is a reaction to a threat, while anxiety is a worry about a potential threat.

If you find yourself feeling stuck in life, this can cause anxiety as you fear being robbed of future happiness. Your fight or flight response sees the threat and so anxiety follows because you fear being stuck in a place of unhappiness within.

Another example is when a person who believes they must be productive with all their time gets anxious when they take a day off. Because the fear of wasting time triggers anxiety in them, they can't relax without feeling guilty. We sometimes forget that rest is productive.

IMMERSED THREAT

Then there is being busy all the time. Immersed in a state of busy. This trickle of cortisol and adrenaline is small but constant. You are always on, struggling to sleep, with your mind in overdrive. In fact, this is why some people have out-of-the-blue panic attacks: due to the constant adrenaline in their system, when they do stop suddenly on a day off they are aware of their rapid heartbeat, think the worst is going to happen and bang, they're in panic mode.

Cortisol is nature's inbuilt alarm system. It is your body's main stress hormone. It works with certain parts of your brain to control your mood, motivation, and fear. It is the alarm system that gets triggered when you feel you are in a scary or dangerous situation. If you find yourself in a busy, overwhelmed state most of the time, trying to keep on top of things, this cortisol is ever present in your system. We are not designed to be constantly operating at high levels of pressure or activity for long periods of time, hence we start to get physical symptoms of stress, not just emotional and mental.

When it came to my story of burnout and anxiety, I never knew how body and mind interacted with each other. I used to think that rest was a waste of time because what's the point of resting when you can work on what you enjoy? I would feel guilty taking time off. I learned the hard way so you don't have to. I never realised that my busy on-the-go lifestyle was generating all this stress in the body and mind that was building up like a pressure cooker only to eventually explode under the pressure in the form of burnout. The subsequent anxiety that was triggered for me would nearly finish me off. My body and mind became consumed with fear and I had to rebuild my mindset. Grasping how the mind and body work and how we spend our time is vitally important.

OUR NERVOUS SYSTEM

Our sympathetic and parasympathetic nervous system are two parts of our nervous system. The **sympathetic nervous system** activates the fight, flight or freeze response during a threat or perceived danger. It prepares you for action. The **parasympathetic nervous system** restores the body to a state of calm and is sometimes referred to as our rest and digest state.

Biologically we are not designed to be on the go all the time, hence we have these different modes that exist for our nervous system. When we are busy all the time we get stuck in a hamster-on-a-wheel scenario and end up just going through the motions of life. Then one day we resurface and look back and think 'what am I doing?' or 'where am I going?' Or worse, we burn out.

THE CYCLE OF FAILING

Gráinne felt like such a failure because she had tried so many times to get healthier but kept stalling. The doctor told her that her blood pressure was up, so she would go off and rejoin the gym, only to stop going a few weeks later. She was in the cycle of starting and then quitting or, as I call it, a cycle of failing. This quitting pattern made her feel like a failure. I asked her why she stopped going each time, what happened?

She explained that as she got busier, she would skip one gym session, then one became two. She would look at her week ahead and think to herself that if she was only going to make one session, what was the point?

With school runs, working a job and taking care of the home, there was no time left. She shared that she felt like she was a bad mum. She was tired all the time, eating all the wrong foods because they were convenient and to top it off, her blood pressure was sky high, putting her at risk of a stroke.

Introducing anything to an already overwhelming schedule will only lead to frustration and most likely failure. The problem then is that we see ourselves as failures and it makes it harder to try again. When you fail enough you then give up even trying to make changes.

Here is a simple actionable technique to reduce stress that we can implement without adding anything to our schedule. It can create more calm and peace in our mind and body to pave the way to getting unstuck. I will share many tools throughout the book that help to combat stress, fear and anxiety, but this is one that doesn't add any more elements into our busy lives. As we know, the seven stages of identity are:

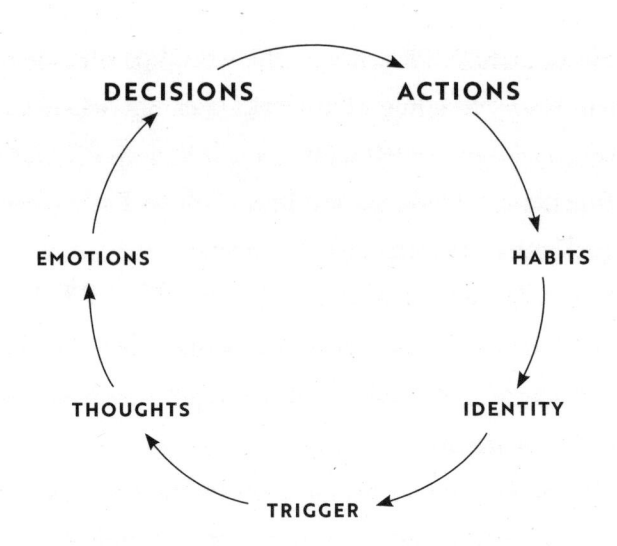

```
         DECISIONS  →  ACTIONS
        ↗                    ↘
   EMOTIONS                HABITS
        ↑                    ↓
   THOUGHTS              IDENTITY
        ↖                    ↙
              TRIGGER
```

I am focusing on our **decisions and actions** in this section. Done repeatedly, our decisions and actions become habits. This exercise will open your eyes to how you spend your most valuable resource: time.

Healthy balance of priorities + self-discipline = time management

EXERCISE ────────────────────────────
A TIME TOOL
STEP ONE: TRACK YOUR WEEK
Take five minutes to yourself and write down your average week Monday through Sunday. Treat it like a timesheet and block off how your time gets spent. Be specific: note whether you get 10

minutes or an hour for lunch. Include realistic times for commuting to work or dropping the kids off. It all goes in here so that you can get a clear, accurate and realistic look into where your time gets spent.

STEP TWO: ASSESS HOW TIME IS SPENT
Now look at this like a detective would look into a robbery. Identify where time is being robbed from you. The tool I use is called: Delegate – Automate – Eliminate.

Is there anything you can delegate? For example, a busy parent could get their children to make their own lunches. Is there anything you can automate? If food shopping takes up a lot of time in your week, then you could automate it by ordering it online so you only have to hit purchase every week. Is there anything you could eliminate? I once had a lawyer come to me who believed that it was impossible to change his schedule around to be more efficient. He then discovered the idea of getting a scooter to work rather than taking his car, which saved him 20 minutes to and from work due to avoiding traffic. This worked out to be about three and a half hours of savings per week which is approximately 150 hours a year (almost a week). Think outside the box and think about small changes, not just large ones.

The littlest of changes can have the greatest significance over long periods.

STEP THREE: ADD IN SUPPORTIVE TASKS

Now that you've hopefully freed up some time, write down up to three things that you would like to start doing and introducing into your week just off to the side of your time schedule. These should be things that help your capacity and positioning for success. These are what I call supportive tasks, because they support your beliefs and values as well as your health and wellness. Here are some suggested prompts to help.

One thing for capacity and mindset:

Something that teaches or inspires you that you can manage weekly or even daily. This is something that helps your mindset. What can you do that opens your mind up to opportunity and growth? For example, it might be taking an online course. It could be planning your goal in bitesize steps. It could be journalling. It might be learning something that you've always wanted to do.

One thing to aid your positioning:

For example, meeting a friend you can brainstorm with or listening to a positive audio book.

Find a place for the task in your schedule on a day and time that you know you can stick to. Then if this goes well for a month or more, introduce another supportive task.

The real key is to be consistent. Creating a new habit is one thing but making time for it is the only way it will ever stick.

What gets measured gets managed.
PETER DRUCKER

For Gráinne, my client who had no time, we realised that it was easier for her to drop the kids off and get a train to work. She could do her emails while travelling on the train, a journey of 30 minutes as opposed to an hour in traffic. This meant that she could actually take an hour for lunch, which she had never had the time to do before. Now that she had the hour, she went to the gym for 30 minutes three times a week during her break. And hey presto, she got her new schedule. If we had tried to fit the gym into a schedule that had no time, like she had done on her previous attempts, it would only have created pressure. This is why looking at your current schedule to get it balanced is key before introducing new tasks.

STEP FOUR: GET IT SCHEDULED

Lots of studies and research over the years have been done on high-performing millionaires and billionaires to find out if there is a constant pattern on how they manage time, family life, their businesses, staff and all that goes with being a very busy person with lots of responsibilities. An article in the *Harvard Business Review* highlighted that to-do lists aren't all that popular. Instead, another technique proved to be the key.

Taking pressure off ourselves sometimes can be done by getting all our tasks and things to do out of our heads and onto a list. This is especially useful when it comes to feeling overwhelmed. The neuroscience tells us that we are better at figuring things out when we write them down, as opposed to letting them simmer in the background in our subconscious. The part of the brain called the limbic system is responsible for emotions. It turns out that writing things down leads to a higher level of thinking when assessing a situation and uses less of the limbic system and more of the prefrontal cortex, which is more suited to problem solving than the limbic emotional centre of our brains. So, writing things down makes it easier to find a solution.

This is why journalling is so good. To-do lists statistically never get completed and give rise to a sense of being overwhelmed when we look at them on their own. They can even create analysis paralysis, meaning that we get paralysed by the mere thought of how much we have to do, resulting in us not doing anything.

You are going to start a written or digital calendar, whatever is easiest. The best type is the one you will have on you or near you most of the time. Every time you think of a task that needs to be done, take out your calendar and find a day and time when you can carry out that task. Every task goes into the calendar, or else you know it is not getting done.

If you don't see any immediate time to slot the task into, move a week or two forward. Now you see a space and in it goes. The reason your life may be stuck right now is because you say yes to everything or simply have bad time management. This new technique will involve you saying: 'I can't do it right now but how does X suit you?' Or it might just be a no if time does not allow.

You are now taking control of your life and acquiring a new life skill – time management. There will always be unpredictable situations and things happening out of the blue and that is perfectly okay, so you are allowed to reschedule things once. When you schedule your time, you might also realise how much you actually do and how it is not possible to keep this level of busyness going long term. It may help you to see that some tasks take far too much time and are not worth it. When you get good at it you will eventually remove the need for to-do lists and simply use your calendar. If there is no room on the calendar, then you can't do it.

STEP FIVE: NON-NEGOTIABLE

This is the part you must stick to. When something gets entered into your diary it becomes non-negotiable, meaning that at that assigned time you will do that task no matter what. Unless there is a medical emergency or family issue, it is getting done. This is how you establish discipline for yourself. Why is this so important? Because things like walking, exercise, reading, hobbies and so on all go into your calendar. Watch how your quality of life improves.

As I mentioned, I had to learn time management the hard way and it was one of the many tools that brought me back from the brink of despair. Making time to rest and switch off never felt very productive but I realised rest and down time *are* very productive – in fact, they are essential. I hear so often how people are busy juggling everything, and I've been there. Regardless of how busy you are, this technique will do four things for you:

1. Lower stress
2. Prevent feeling overwhelmed
3. Raise quality of life
4. Build balance

> **Consistency always trumps occasional brilliance.**

As we transition to Part two, you hopefully are better equipped. Part one of the book is a macro view. Now let's go through each area of your life so we can create the life you so desire and absolutely deserve.

PART TWO
The solutions to stuck

CHAPTER 7

The types of stuck

CLARITY IS KEY

In life, it's common to find ourselves in a state of being stuck. It could be a temporary situation or something that persists for a long time. Perhaps it has been there your whole life, this feeling that you are always struggling to have the life that seems to come naturally to others. Maybe you feel that you aren't enough, and you've always felt less than others. Or maybe you've struggled to fit in and gelling with the crowd doesn't come easy.

When you find yourself stuck, you are very much like a wheel missing a crucial spoke. This feeling of being immobilised is something that touches us all. However, it's not the sensation of being stuck that defines us; it's our response to it.

Picture a bicycle wheel. Each spoke represents a different facet of our life – our work, relationships, passions, and dreams. When all the spokes are intact and in harmony, the wheel rolls smoothly. But when one spoke goes missing or is damaged, the wheel wobbles, and progress becomes challenging. The bike starts to drift in a direction you don't wish to go.

BICYCLE WHEEL

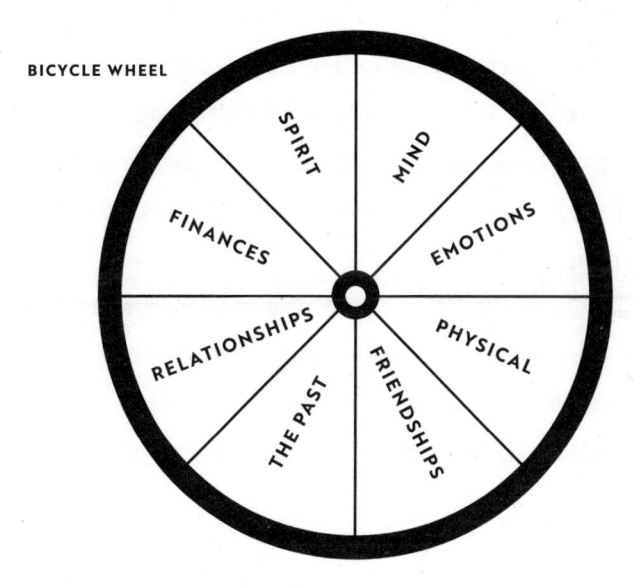

[Diagram of a wheel divided into eight segments labeled: SPIRIT, MIND, EMOTIONS, PHYSICAL, FRIENDSHIPS, THE PAST, RELATIONSHIPS, FINANCES]

Feeling stuck is the nagging awareness that something essential is out of alignment, that we've drifted away from our core values. That something is missing. Yes, there are other good spokes but this one is pulling us. It's in these moments of imbalance that we must turn to our values as our guiding compass.

Values are the unchanging constants in our ever-evolving lives. They define who we are, what we cherish, and what we stand for. When life feels stagnant, our values beckon us to return to our true selves.

Imagine a wheel with all its spokes firmly in place, representing a life in perfect harmony with your values. Each rotation moves you closer to fulfilment and authenticity. By realigning your actions with your values, you regain the power to overcome the stagnation that holds you captive. Like a new wheel that is aligned, it makes you move in the direction you want to go with less internal resistance.

The pursuit of change can seem daunting, but it's also a liberating endeavour. It begins with acknowledging the feeling of being stuck and summoning the courage to confront it. Define your goals in alignment with your values and take deliberate steps towards them.

Ultimately, being stuck in one area of life is an invitation to rebalance your wheel. Your values are the steady points on which you can anchor your course. They assure you that, like a wheel missing a spoke, you can regain balance and keep moving forward, one revolution at a time.

Seven stages of identity

The seven stages of identity will also be a tool in your arsenal for dealing with whatever stuck state you are in. This framework highlights the path that defines our identity. From a trigger/situation/event all the way through to establishing the beliefs and values that form our identity. As discussed in chapter 2, the seven stages of identity are:

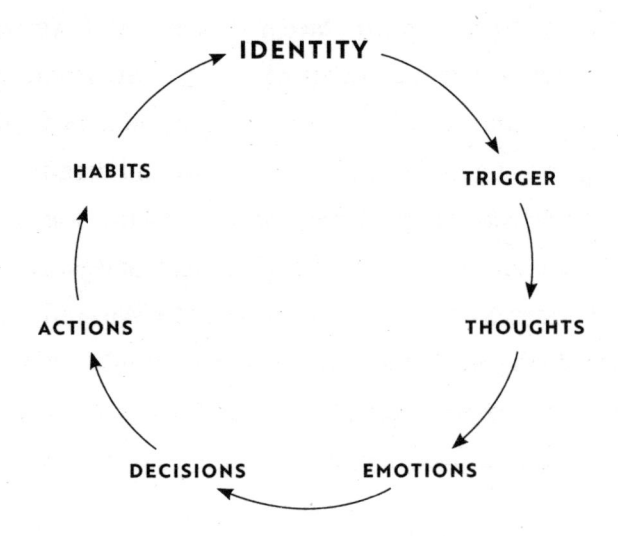

IDENTITY → TRIGGER → THOUGHTS → EMOTIONS → DECISIONS → ACTIONS → HABITS → IDENTITY

People often come to me feeling overwhelmed, not knowing where to begin, and this framework is a helpful approach to finding out where intervention is possible. Then together we strategise a solution and plan of action. This targeted approach enables us to develop a plan to regain control and move forward.

How we will help you work through your stuck:
1. We will use the type of stuck as a theme or reference point with case studies.
2. We will use the seven stages of identity to show how stuck manifests and can be resolved.
3. Each chapter will have tools to use and apply.

HOW TO KNOW WHAT TYPE OF STUCK YOU ARE

Let's dive deep into this frustrating, saddening and sometimes demoralising feeling of being stagnant in life and find the solutions to break through it.

Imagine going to a doctor with a complaint. You walk in saying, 'Doc, I have no energy and I'm constantly tired.' The doctor doesn't just hand you a random pill and hope for the best. They start asking questions, running tests and digging into the root cause of your fatigue. They want to prescribe the right treatment, tailored specifically to your needs. The same goes for getting unstuck – there's no one-size-fits-all solution. We need to identify the root of why you are feeling this way. We will look at your situation from different angles and like a doctor running tests, we will see what is the root cause and best solutions for you.

Reflect on your own life and use the tools and tactics from stories I share to pinpoint where you need a little more understanding. It's okay if you feel stuck in multiple areas – we'll tackle them one by one. It's also okay if there is no obvious root cause, the tools work either way.

The main types of stuck

MENTALLY STUCK – OVERTHINKING AND WORRYING

A negative mindset or frame of mind that you are stuck in. A mind fixed on a limiting belief based on the past or present. A thought pattern that doesn't serve you well. Not knowing any alternative to the negative mindset you are in and overthinking a lot. Thinking that brings you unrest.

EMOTIONALLY STUCK – TRAPPED FEELING THIS WAY

When you experience a certain negative emotional state most of the time. An emotional reaction or feeling you wish you could change but don't know how.

PHYSICALLY STUCK – WHEN YOU HAVE NO CONTROL

Feeling stuck or limited due to an injury, a sickness or diagnosis. A belief that due to physical limitations you are less than others and your potential is cut short. When something physical impacts your life negatively. This can also be frustration and disappointment due to the physical location one is based in.

RELATIONALLY STUCK – LOVE AND SEX

A feeling of stuck and despair in relation to romantic relationships or other interpersonal relationships with friends or family. A sense that you are stuck due to others.

INTERPERSONALLY STUCK – FRIENDS AND FRENEMIES
Feeling like you don't get the proper respect and support from your friendships.

HISTORICALLY STUCK – WHEN THE PAST STILL CONTROLS YOU
Feeling stuck in the past. Labelled with people's perception of the old you even though you have changed. Not being able to move on as an individual due to your past history.

FINANCIALLY STUCK – MONEY AND MINDSET
Due to financial issues, you experience a sense of stuck and do not know how to break out of it. When your view of money is holding you back from what you feel you could achieve.

SPIRITUALLY STUCK – WHEN YOU AREN'T HAPPY WITHIN
Internal unrest. A great disconnect between your true inner self and your external life. A sense that you are not flowing or agreeing with how life is or who you are becoming. Not living as your true authentic self. An issue of identity.

A lot of the time you may identify with elements from each type of stuck and this is normal. For example, a person who is frustrated and sad because they haven't met their special someone yet will feel relationally stuck along with emotionally stuck due to not having a connection. Every type of stuck leads to an element of internal unrest in your thinking and it can manifest itself physically in the body with symptoms like headaches or tension.

LIFE ASSESSMENT

Think of your life as the bicycle wheel we mentioned earlier. Each spoke is important, shaping who you are and influencing your overall sense of satisfaction. Here's the crux of the matter: when one or more of these spokes becomes loose, a lingering feeling of dissatisfaction creeps in.

Let's take a moment to reflect on your work, for instance. If the mere thought of stepping into your job fills you with dread, it's time to pay attention. The initial dislike you feel can morph into a profound loathing, poisoning your spirit and leaving you embittered.

Identifying the exact source of discontentment isn't always a straightforward task. That's where a powerful tool, a life assessment, comes into play. It empowers you to uncover those hidden areas that may be hindering your journey towards true fulfilment. This assessment will guide you to pinpoint the specific domains – perhaps even multiple ones – that are causing your dissatisfaction. It's time to seize control of your life and transform those lacklustre areas into ones that make you smile.

Step one:

Look at the list of life areas below and score each of them from 1 to 10. Score them by how satisfied you are in that area of your life, with 1 being the lowest and 10 being the highest.

For example, maybe you are reasonably healthy, but you would like to quit smoking so health might be a 5. Or maybe you are pretty satisfied with your friends, but sometimes you feel that they don't fully support you. They love you and you love them, but clearly it's not ideal. Maybe for you they are a 6. This doesn't mean they are bad or that you should drop them. It might highlight you could do with a friend who is your supporter. Maybe someone in the current group is that person and investing in that friendship could be a solution, or you might be open to making a new friend by seeking out opportunities to connect with new people.

The areas are:

- Family
- Friends
- Health
- Rest
- Work/career
- Finances/savings
- Romantic relationship
- Hobbies
- Recreation/social life
- Home environment
- Work environment
- Personal growth

Step two:

From the above list of scores I want you to identify the lowest scored area. If there are two matching low scores that's perfectly fine. This score indicates that you are least satisfied with this particular area (or areas) in your life. We are going to use that score and start there with the objective of helping you to be more satisfied in that area of your life.

We don't tend to look at our lives in sections and this is partly the problem. When we break things down it is less overwhelming and a more constructive bitesize approach.

Side note: Whenever you are going through anything in life and lack clarity or feel overwhelmed, break it down for yourself into bitesize pieces. This can be a great help in plotting a course for change. Whenever I have a massive task like an event I am organising or even writing this book, I break it down and then it is manageable and easier to comprehend.

Step three:

It is about this point a person will typically say: 'I love that I have identified that area and it is a big help. But Mark, I have no clue how to make it better so that I can be more satisfied with it. What do I do?'

My response is this. Even though you don't know the way to be more satisfied and make things better, I need you to have a little hope. There is always a way, even when it feels like there isn't. You will read true-life stories of clients who got through and out of what would appear to be impossible scenarios of being stuck. Step three is the decision to open your thinking and open your mind to opportunities that will bring about the change you desire, even if it is minor. One per cent is better than nothing when it comes to improvement.

Step four:

Here are some questions that will help you gain further clarity on what steps you can take. Answer them in order. I will also share two examples so you can have a greater understanding.

Friends example: I don't feel respected or liked as much as other friends in the group.

Career example: I don't like my job.

1. What is stopping you from feeling more satisfied in the area that you scored the lowest?
   Answer: _____
   Friends: They don't respect me as much as they do my other friends.
   Career: I wish I had a job I enjoyed more.

2. How would you like to feel when you think about this area?
   Answer: _____
   Friends: I wish I felt respected and liked.
   Career: I wish I felt happier and more motivated.

3. What would you need to believe in order to feel this way?
   Answer: _____
   Friends: I would need to believe they treat me equally.
   Career: I would need to believe that my job was enjoyable.

4. Try to identify a thinking pattern that shows up. This could be a sign of a limiting belief.
   Answer: _____
   Friends: I constantly check to see if I fit in and worry about not being included.

Career: I am afraid if I leave this job, I might never find a job I like.

5. Where did you learn this belief? Has it shown up before in life in separate situations?
   Answer: _____
   Friends: In school I was rejected by a best friend once, and I fear rejection happening again.
   Career: My upbringing. I've always taken the first job I could get for fear of not having one, as my family struggled financially and I hated that as a child.

6. What is the benefit to believing this belief? How does it influence you?
   Answer: _____
   Friends: There is no benefit and it makes me paranoid.
   Career: Fear makes me work hard to keep a job I don't enjoy.

7. What is this belief costing you?
   Answer: _____
   Friends: I am distrustful and find it hard to trust people.
   Career: I have a lack of fulfilment with my job.

8. How does this belief make you feel when you think about it?
   Answer: _____
   Friends: When I think about it, I realise it is not right and it makes me unhappy.
   Career: I wonder why am I wasting my life in a job I hate.

9. If you didn't have this belief and could change it, would it be worth it to you?
   Answer: _____
   Friends: Yes. I would relax more and enjoy time with my friends.
   Career: Yes. I would look for a job I love and give myself a chance to find it.

10. What would be a better, healthier, more empowering belief?
    Answer: _____
    Friends: I take my friendships at face value. I'll stop overthinking them and be more present. How my friends treat me is not a measure of my self-worth or value.
    Career: I deserve to have a job I love and not let fear hold me in one I hate.

11. Put into words how this new healthier belief will work for you.
    Answer: _____
    Friends: I could stop interpreting bad communication as rejection, and if I feel left out I could say it in a nice way. True friends will understand. Give grace with my friends as they aren't going to be perfect. But as long as I can trust them and they are there for me that's ok. Not everyone will have the same standards of trust as me and I will be closer to some more than others.
    Career: I deserve a job I love and will start focusing on what I can do to get it. I may not like every area of it but if I love it 80% of the time that's a win. I will learn skills I may need and not be afraid to put myself out there.

12. What can you do today to start this change?
Answer: _____

Friends: I am going to arrange a girls' night and work on building friendship and showing them love. I will also be more open to new friendships, understanding that trust takes time to build for me.

Career: I am going to update my CV and get professional career advice.

Treat these questions like prompts and put a little thought into answering them. Take your time, get yourself a cup of coffee and give it 15 minutes to see what needs to be changed. When we start to shift our mindset, writing things down can bring great clarity. If you had more than one area, pick one and start there. Then pick the next area you are least satisfied with, then the next and so forth, working from the least to the most satisfied. There are always areas we can work on and the biggest mistake we can make is accepting a position of hopelessness. There is always hope and change is always possible, as you will see in the coming chapters. Get a life coach if you want to speed things up, but either way don't stay there. The results you can achieve in six months or a year are mind-blowing. You'll be glad you took the time to invest in you.

Investing in yourself will always yield a profit.

CHAPTER 8
Mentally stuck: overthinking and worrying

STUCK IN OUR THOUGHTS

There are three main ways we can get stuck in our thoughts: being stuck replaying the past, stuck dwelling on the present and stuck worrying about what might happen in the future. If you get trapped worrying or stressing it can result in overthinking things and finding it hard to stop. We will deal more with being stuck replaying the past in chapter 13, but this chapter is for the overthinker, the worrier and anyone who gets stuck in their head about things.

Even if you feel you are not an overthinker, you need this chapter. Whether we realise it or not, we are constantly thinking about and visualising who we are. Maybe you are aware of this or maybe you are not. However, if you are stuck, I guarantee your thinking is partly at fault. You will discover how to control, manage and focus your mindset so that it helps rather than hinders you.

Every day we live according to how we see ourselves. We are unconsciously meditating on beliefs and values. As you progress through this chapter, whether you are aware of your overthinking or not, you will discover whether the things you think about most are helpful or destructive to you and your identity.

Overthinking is a bad habit and a method of trying to control and protect yourself and your loved ones against potential harm. I've helped countless people break the habit of being stuck in their thoughts. Those same people often ask me how I know so much about overthinking and being psychologically stuck. I can personally attest to the power of overthinking. I was once stuck overthinking to the extent that I nearly couldn't take it anymore. I learned what works through my own experience not just through what psychology and neuroscience taught me. It nearly destroyed my life during a period of health anxiety, consuming me for almost two years. So when I talk about overthinking, I speak from personal experience, knowing how debilitating it can be. I also speak from a place of recovery, as I know that there is a way to overcome it.

Are you an overthinker?

Overthinking has one guarantee: you'll feel worse after it.

There are lots of things that can cause us to get stuck in our heads. Some thoughts are harmless, while others are more harmful. A song that sticks in our head all day as an annoying ear worm is relatively harmless, but what do we do when instead of a song stuck in your head it is a situation, image or thought that conjures up negative feelings? Maybe these thoughts cause us to experience a sense of worry, anxiety, fear, anger, frustration, sadness, overwhelm or pain. The thoughts have stuck in our minds because of what they represent to us, because of their meaning. It might be a worrying series of thoughts about our health, our finances or our family. We can't focus and we find it hard to be present. We have this niggling in the back of our minds, this thought demanding our attention even when we try to distract ourselves. The reason we struggle to ignore these thoughts is because of how we are reacting to them emotionally. This difficulty to stop overthinking is called ruminating – the repetitive thinking or dwelling on negative thoughts and feelings of distress, and their causes and consequences.

Overthinking is like trying to tie your shoelace without using your hands.

Overthinking and rumination can even affect you physically if they are present for long enough or if they become a regular habit. You may experience:

- Insomnia and struggles with sleep
- Tension headaches
- Stiff muscles
- Fatigue
- Emotional eating
- Inability to be fully present
- Becoming easily agitated
- Anxiety
- Feeling like there is a knot in your stomach
- Loss of appetite
- Irritable bowel syndrome
- Weight gain

Overthinking is like a labyrinth of thoughts, trapping our minds. It stems from the unpredictability of outcomes, threatening what we value. It is important to note that we value whatever is very important to us, and when we feel that something threatens that, we react to it. This is why certain people have heightened reactions to what might appear small to someone else: because not everyone's values are the same. It can be a threat to our job, our finances, our family, our dream, our goal or even a threat to our public image or persona. There are so many things we value in life that, when threatened, will trigger a reaction. We get triggered if something arises that is similar to a past situation that caused us harm before. This can set off a sequence of thoughts because 'what if' it happens again like it did before? We try to predict the future based on those past experiences. Or maybe we are overthinking a lump because Google said it might be cancer, and this obviously threatens what we value most: our lives. The fact that we knew someone who did die from cancer only exacerbates the ruminations. Seeking reassurance, we fall into a rabbit hole of fears and worries, losing ourselves in exaggerated possibilities, putting a spotlight on our flaws and failures and ultimately feeding our lack of self belief.

Sometimes a limiting belief is being stuck believing something about ourselves that impacts us negatively. It may affect our confidence or outlook in life. It may not be a thought we have all the time, but a series of thoughts that can be triggered when a situation arises in life. It might be a thought of imposter syndrome, or something like 'I'm always left out of things', or 'everyone is better at this than me', and in our mind we put the spotlight on our limiting belief or negative self-beliefs.

Catastrophic thinking

At times you might experience a never-ending cycle of playing out scenarios in your mind, fearing the worst possible outcome. You wish you could stop, but the thoughts keep coming back, like a relentless boomerang.

This phenomenon, often referred to as catastrophic thinking, involves fixating on thoughts that lead to imagining the worst catastrophic outcomes. It's like creating problems that don't even exist in reality. Interestingly, studies in science have shown that the majority of what we worry about never actually happens. In fact, it's estimated that about 85% of our fears are unfounded.

Overthinking, or rumination, is fuelled by our perspective and reaction to the thoughts or scenarios that we believe could happen. This triggers an emotional and even physical response within us. Overthinking often becomes a habit over time. If you're an overthinker, you've probably said the phrase 'I overthink everything.' It can stem from various reasons, and here are a few common ones, listed in no particular order. Can you identify with any?

INSECURITY

Scared we won't be able to cope with certain outcomes due to our own self-belief and abilities.

UNCERTAINTY

Fear of the unknown and not knowing what will happen. An outcome we cannot plan for.

FEELING OVERWHELMED

Many things going on and we are trying to process it all for fear we won't get things done or we won't be able. Mentally spinning many plates.

THE FIXER

We are natural fixers and when a problem arises, we can't rest till we have it figured out and solved.

FEAR

Fear of what will happen you or loved ones. Afraid of a real or imagined impending threat.

FEAR OF RUMINATION

Fear of not being able to stop overthinking. This fear of not being able to stop thinking about something actually fuels overthinking further as a person can feel even more upset.

ANXIETY AND ME

My experiece of collapsing in the gym showed me how powerful fear is when one of the things you value most in the world, your life, is under threat and you can't do anything about it. I am highlighting my story because the fundamental it explains is massively helpful in getting unstuck. When fear enters in and we are knocked in life, the ramifications can echo our whole lifetime if the situation is left unresolved. One thing I have identified as a common thread in stories of people who are stuck is the fact that once fear comes into our lives on a level we are not ready for, it can send ripples through our lives and even our very identity. You may have once seen yourself as a strong person but that knock you experienced showed you that you aren't bulletproof.

For me, the mention of heart attack gave me so much fear because for the first time in my life I was faced with my own mortality. Even though I was given the all-clear a couple of days later, the experience set in motion a chronic anxiety disorder that I thought would finish me off. It was triggered by fear, then fuelled by overthinking and ruminating. As I lay in the hospital in this state of panic, these waves of anxiety would come over me. They were such an uncomfortable feeling of dread. I didn't even know these were anxiety attacks, I just knew I hated them. There I was, a guy who loved extreme sports, challenges and pushing the bar, but now feeling so afraid. It rocked me to my core; it shook my identity.

I have seen so many people that experienced a situation or scenario that opened the door to fear, and their thinking was never the same. It works like this: you are put into a situation that causes you great fear because you aren't in control. Maybe as a child or teen, maybe it is a toxic environment due to other people, or a reaction to fears reported in the media. There are hundreds of scenarios that cause fear to knock at the door. For me, it was when my body failed me. My body decided to collapse in the gym, and I couldn't do anything to stop it. But it wasn't just the collapse; it was the fact that this could happen to me. It freaked me out, but the fear went up tenfold when the doctors suspected it to be my heart. I'd never had an experience like this in my life before, and so the mind and body went into alarm mode. It makes for the perfect incubator for high anxiety.

I returned home from hospital a few days later but I didn't realise that I was bringing this new health anxiety with me. I didn't even know that was what you called it. This was when I started overthinking. My mind was on full alert to protect me from collapsing again (not that it could stop me collapsing, but it was in a triggered state of hypersensitivity). So as time progressed, I was hugely aware of my health; any sensation, pain, tiredness or light-headedness made me think the worst. What if my body was failing me again for some other reason? The mind's primary default position is to protect you from any threat, real or otherwise, so that's why we see the negative in things before we see the positive. The mind is trained to focus on perceived threats, so it zones in on the negatives. I was so hypersensitive to my bodily sensations because of my prior experience and how it traumatised me.

For example, when I felt normal light-headedness from jumping up suddenly, I would immediately reach the conclusion it was my heart and that maybe the doctors missed something. This created massive anxiety. Things that I would never even have given a second thought to became obsessions I would Google and seek to resolve. For the first few weeks after my collapse, I had anxiety so high that my hands would tingle. I felt nauseous and I had chest pain to contend with (caused by muscle strain, not my heart, but my chronic health anxiety wouldn't accept that).

Fear wants to grow and over time the ruminations became worse. I was now not just obsessing over my health, but also feeling afraid of everything. It went from health to social anxiety, and I was anxious in so many scenarios that I could fill a book with all the variations I experienced. The overthinking was the hardest battle to fight because it was in my head. Here is how I beat it and through beating it I beat the fear and anxiety. These next few pages are vital reading if you are stuck in your thoughts a lot.

The fear would create a 'what if' scenario. I liken overthinking to a TV show with endless episodes. The fearful 'what if' plays out in our head with new scenarios and outcomes. The reason we tire is also important. When triggered we go into an emotional state like anxiety, panic, worry, anger or fear. When we are left sitting with the trigger and if nothing further happens our heightened emotional state lowers back down in intensity. It starts to trigger you less and less because your brain eventually realises that there is no need to panic. However, in my case of anxiety, when one 'what if' would lower in intensity, another would come in.

My overthinking went like this: What if that pain is my heart? What if the doctors missed something? What if it is serious? What if I faint while at a party? The pain would subside after a few days so I would conclude that things were okay, alarm over. But then what about parties, what about meeting people! What if I got light-headed while out and nobody was there with me? Now I was hypersensitive while out of the house and this became a new rumination that had me yearning to stay at home. On and on it would go.

But thoughts weren't the main issue; it was the pattern that I was stuck in – ruminating on fearful scenarios and outcomes. Notice below how the collapse started to convince me that I had everything to fear. It created in me a false fearful identity that just didn't line up with who I was. I found this so sad to deal with. Here is what happened to me:

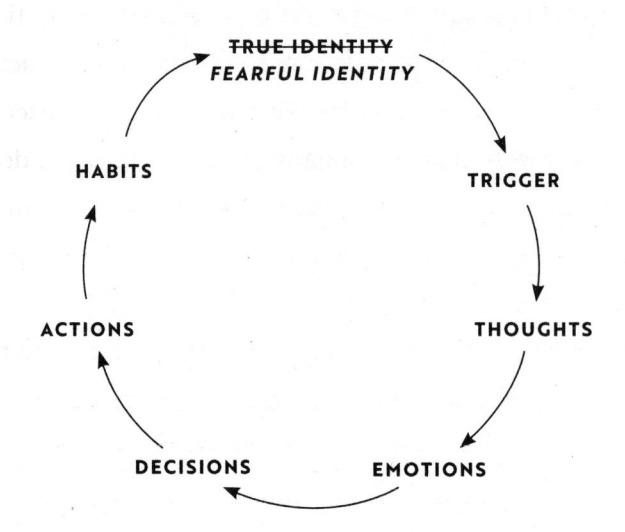

~~TRUE IDENTITY~~
FEARFUL IDENTITY

→ TRIGGER → THOUGHTS → EMOTIONS → DECISIONS → ACTIONS → HABITS →

Being in an anxious state of fear, I saw everything through anxiety goggles, always seeing the danger in things. I never knew about any of the solutions that I am sharing in this book until I learned them the hard way. I didn't have an identity strong enough to carry me through those early days, so I was at the mercy of anxiety. I felt hopeless and defeated until one day I had a glimpse of being free of anxiety. I was holding my newborn nephew and I was so focused on him that anxiety left. It wasn't until I handed him back I realised that for the first time in a long time I was focused on him and not anxiously living in my head. This proved that if my attention and focus is on something I love it distracts me away from anxiety almost automatically. I now had hope.

I started telling myself I can, I will, I must get through this. I got to a place where I just wanted the old me back. But little did I realise the old me would never return, and I am glad of that, because what I discovered made me a stronger and wiser person than I ever was before. I stopped searching on Google and started to research and study anxiety, fear and mindsets. Over the two years that followed, I put my coach hat on as if I was coaching a client, except the client was me. This gave me some disconnect from the anxiety-filled emotional state. I then began to do what I do with a client except that my focus was mental health, not professional performance. I created my why and wrote it down (as I explained in chapter 3). I set a goal; to be a person in control of their thoughts and not live in fear or be anxious all the time. I then needed solutions in the event of being triggered.

AWARENESS

There is a way to break the habit of overthinking and the first step is awareness. By observing without being consumed, you can find freedom. Viewing your sensations and thoughts as if you are a bystander to someone else's overthinking helps you to disconnect from the emotion of the thoughts and better process them. You cannot simply turn off the thinking because it has you engaged. But being so caught up in the worry or the anger, your emotions fuel your decisions and actions. For example, if it is a health worry, you take to Google to try diagnosing pain, only to go down the rabbit hole that eventually leads you to think you are dying. Maybe it's a friendship concern and so you search through socials to find out if your friends went to that party without you. You try to reassure yourself and this is why you search for comfort, trying to predict an outcome so that you can be ready for it or give yourself some thread of hope that maybe it's not the catastrophic outcome that your thoughts are pointing to.

THE THREE OUTCOMES

Overthinking happens because we are emotionally reacting to an imagined negative outcome. The way to stop overthinking, in theory, is to stop the emotional reaction and all would be well. Your mind would think up a 'what if' and then simply cast it aside. But this is very hard to do, especially if something you love is under threat. So what can you do? The key is to present alternate endings to the story and imagine an alternative emotional state. Every time you start overthinking or ruminating, present yourself with three outcomes:

Outcome one (the hopeful outcome)

What if, whenever life throws a curve ball, you were ready to hit it? The hopeful outcome is this internal reassurance that no matter what comes your way, you trust that you will get through it. You will be okay. When pain or struggle overwhelms us, we don't know how long it will last. But we can say the words 'this too will pass'. Hope is not giving up, it is about adopting an attitude that it will be okay someday. The hopeful outcome is an internal faith that you will be happy again if you don't give up. Hope says you might be knocked down but you're not out. For me, I held onto the hope that I would be able to have peace and be happy again. I never gave up on that hope and it carried me through.

Outcome two (the best outcome)

Considering the best outcome means considering that there is just as much of a chance of good happening as there is of bad happening. I have often seen clients default to the worst-case scenario, which is what we all tend to do until we create enough self-awareness to intervene. We spend a lot of time in our heads trying to predict the worst. But a good exercise is to force yourself to create a good outcome. This might mean imagining things going well. Another thing that I like to do is to tell a client who has a worrying experience in life coming up to imagine what they are going to do if the news is bad. Focus on what happens afterwards. For example, after the confrontational meeting, they could go for a swim, to the gym or treat themselves to some retail therapy. This creates thoughts with subsequent emotions that can help them to see past the ensuing meeting. It's basically forcing yourself to imagine a good outcome. You are showing yourself that you will get past this thing and life will continue. In my case, the best outcome would be helping people to have a life that perhaps they didn't think was possible. I would imagine myself helping and speaking with clients, groups and teams, helping them to get through their challenges. I would do this when I was overcome with anxiety and it would give me focus, and also a goal. It distracted me from the horrible anxious state with positive emotions.

Outcome three (the nothing outcome)

Lastly, what if nothing happens?! How would I feel then? The nothing outcome would mean that I would relax and feel relief. So I asked myself, 'How can I get this sense of relief and relaxation now, as this is clearly what I am seeking?'

As part of my interruption to a rumination, I did things that would relax me, because I ruminated less when I was relaxed and less stressed. Having peace was the outcome I truly wanted so I got busy generating this state for myself.

The key with the three outcomes is to utilise all of them but to lean into the one that helps you best.

STUCK BEING AFRAID

What is it you ruminate on? Rumination is an indication that you fear one of your values is under threat. Is it your job, your health, a relationship, your weight, or an opportunity?

It is not the actual loss that is the problem. The real issue is what the loss means to us. We can't see past it, and we feel that we won't be able to survive it. Losing a job might mean losing security, a certain lifestyle and plans for the future. Loss of health might mean not being able to do things or feeling life is over. Relationship issues might give us a fear of being alone forever. Not being able to control our weight makes us feel powerless, even unlovable.

Whatever situation we fear, we have attached meaning to the outcome. It is that meaning that usually underpins our emotional investment in it.

FOUR COMMON FEARS that can cause us to overthink:

1. **FEAR OF FAILURE** (failing in public or failing in private; disappointing someone or ourselves).
2. **FEAR OF LOSS** (losing something or someone we love, losing out on an opportunity in life).
3. **FEAR OF REJECTION** (rejection by friends, society, family, partner, kids, boss, colleagues).
4. **FEAR OF PAIN/DISCOMFORT** (experiencing physical pain or emotional pain).

We care so much about preventing a negative outcome that we can't stop thinking about it. But let me ask you this: Who is in charge of your life? Is fear in charge? Is fear in charge so much that it tells you what to do and think? Fear is what causes us to overthink. Fear is so powerful, but only when we listen to it. Fear is a dominant emotional state if we allow it to be. But what if you allowed courage to coexist with fear? Now what? I know that you have a tolerance and toughness within you that you would probably be surprised to realise existed. I have seen enough people face fear with courage to know that. I was so crippled with anxiety that I would stay awake at night ruminating until I took back control by using the three outcomes – especially the courageous outcome one: I will get through this, don't give up on hope. A day at a time.

Whatever your goals and dreams are, whatever you overthink about, never let fear or another human take your dream away from you. They don't have the right to.

No one can take away your dream without your consent.

Fear will rob you of your potential and time if you allow it to hit play on the 'what if' box set. Maybe at this stage in your life, fear and anxiety have taken enough time and happiness away that you have had enough of it. Maybe it's comparison that ruins your day as you compare yourself to others. Maybe you've been stuck in a state of fear for far too long. I say that now is the time to take your life back. It is not about being fearless, it is about being brave. Courage is pressing forward in spite of the fear. What is the key to fighting fear? The answer is hope.

HANG ON IN THERE

We overthink because we are looking for the certainty that what we fear is not going to happen – certainty that it's going to be okay. Lack of certainty and the unknown is what drives overthinking with fear.

Nothing is ever certain, only what we know right here and now in this very moment.

How do we get certainty? What is the certainty we are looking for? It is quite simple. We are looking for the certainty that we will be okay because the fear makes us feel it won't be okay. If we can't ever get to a place of certainty, how will we ever find peace? So much of our certainty is dependent on other people, other things outside of our control. This is why some people love control; it makes them feel safe. A Latin term sums up a better way of living: *amor fati*, 'love of fate'. It means learning to accept that whatever comes your way, whether good or bad, is part of your path. It is knowing that this threat is not designed to stop you but instead to push you on. Don't resist it – accept it has happened, take a moment to process, and keep stepping forward. I've had clients and people I know personally experience horrific ordeals that no human should ever go through. But if you can just keep going a day at a time, the hope is so powerful. You don't ever have certainty, but there is comfort and peace when you choose to know that whatever comes your way, you won't give up and you will get through it.

Whatever difficulties you experience, you will survive them. Even when you feel that a challenge may be more than you can handle and you have nothing to hold onto – I say hold onto hope, my outcome number one.

Hope is a belief that you can survive whatever life throws at you, whatever the odds. Hope is not having all the answers or solutions to this challenge, but a determination to survive it with the hope that you can make it. The hope that good days are still possible. When you remind yourself of that you give yourself back control of the situation. You cannot control what happens but you can control two things if bad things do happen: how you respond and what you do next.

EXERCISE
THE OVERTHINKING TOOLBOX
Step one: process how you feel

Take the approach that you are observing yourself. This helps to distance you from the emotional overload. Take note of your feelings and thoughts. Even writing them down can help hugely (journalling). Using the XYZ tool (discussed in chapter 1) is another help to processing. Don't ignore how you feel, just don't sit with it for too long. Don't let ruminations just whizz on by in the background. The process of writing out what you are fearing or thinking about can help you gain perspective. Take the approach of observing your thoughts and emotions as if you were a coach listening to a client.

Step two: fact or fiction

Everything is fiction until it is fact. Remind yourself that this is in your mind, it's not reality.

Step three: how you react – the three outcomes

Break the cycle of worry and overthinking using the three outcomes. This step is like a fire extinguisher to overthinking and works to change your state and mindset.

Step four: identity of hope

Lean on hope. Base this hope in your identity. Become the hopeful person you need to be. Look to the past when you survived things that at the time felt overwhelming. Show yourself that you are a survivor, and choose to hold onto hope. Hope says that even when there is no knowing what gift tomorrow may bring, hope is always a choice.

Encourage yourself in the knowledge that whatever you face, you'll get through. Use the tool of the success circles in chapter 3. You can survive bad stuff because you have done it before.

> **Hope never quits. Hope never stops. Hope never fails.**

Regardless of whatever happens to you, even if you lose what you value – you can still choose hope in every scenario. Be your best, do your best and if things don't work out, hope will carry you forward. Just don't give up on you. One day life will eventually come to an end for real, and you won't get a say about when that is. So why worry about that day when the reality is that you are alive today? That is what hope taught me.

I love this quote:

> **Failure is not falling down; it is when you refuse to get back up.**
> **THOMAS EDISON**

Everyone will fall down, fail at things and make mistakes. We don't want it to happen, but it is a necessary part of life if we want to grow. If you want to be successful, be prepared to make mistakes. Having hope is your inner voice that says: this is horrible, but I'll be okay. Even the worst outcomes don't mean the end for you.

When we catch ourselves overthinking, we need to interrupt our emotional response. This goes back to mindset, which I spoke about in chapter 3, and how we can choose to imagine, think, say or do things that generate the emotional state that is preferable, rather than just accepting the worst-case scenario that may play automatically. Tell yourself how there is just as much of a chance of a brilliant outcome as a nothing outcome. Remind yourself that irrespective of the outcome you will decide to live in the hope that you will get through it.

Step five: you are in charge

Be mindful that you are in charge. You decide what happens next. Fear or anger can try to influence you to do a certain thing or react a certain way when you are triggered. But you still have a choice in what you do. You are in charge even when rumination, anxiety, fear or anger try to control your thinking. You can still choose what you do and how to respond.

When I get an emergency call and an unforeseen problem appears, I always say to myself, 'There is a way through this, I just need to figure it out.' That is what hope tells us: there is always a way out.

CHAPTER 9

Emotionally stuck: trapped feeling this way

TAKING CHARGE OF YOUR EMOTIONS

Many of us have accepted our emotional state as a fact of life. We've become so accustomed to feeling a certain way that we believe it's part of our identity. This is what it means to be emotionally stuck.

But have you ever challenged yourself and your current state of being? Have you ever decided that you don't like how you feel and made a conscious choice to change it?

Perhaps deep down, there's anger that occasionally erupts when you feel disrespected. Maybe there's a profound sadness due to a loss, and on unexpected days, it washes over you like a wave, engulfing you in darkness. Or it could be a constant sense of fear, a knot in your stomach and a lingering feeling of anxiety that weighs on your shoulders. Or maybe you have a poor self-image or low self-esteem because of how you feel you look, your weight, your job or how your life has panned out.

If I were to ask you what you feel most of the time, would it be joy or sadness, enjoyment or dissatisfaction, contempt or lack of purpose, happiness or anger, peace or guilt?

In this chapter, we'll explore a more comprehensive list of emotions and how you can define and understand them through a feelings log. Whether we're aware of it or not, we experience emotions throughout the day, to varying degrees of intensity. For many of us, discovering our own thoughts and emotions is uncharted territory. If you're currently facing real challenges, studying on your own may take time. To help get clarity and develop a plan, I always recommend seeking professional help from someone with the experience and expertise, particularly if you are struggling to get the change you want.

WHAT CAUSES EMOTIONS?

Emotions are reactions that generally occur from the following:

- A physical event
- A social interaction
- Imagining a future situation
- Replaying a past experience

But the thing about emotions is they are unpredictable in how long they stay around, and two people can react differently to the same thing. I get asked all the time, 'How long until I won't feel like this anymore, Mark?' The answer unfortunately is the same for everyone: it takes as long as it takes, and it is different for every individual. However, the good news is emotions are changeable regardless of how long it may take. We can take charge of our emotions to the extent that we don't have to stay in the state of whatever the negative emotion is that we don't want to feel.

There is a multitude of reasons for the kinds of emotions we feel, from upbringing to life experiences, and culture to societal factors. Any and all of these things condition us and therefore influence how we respond to certain events or situations. You could spend a lot of time investigating the gamut of why a person feels the way they do, and you still may come out the other side unsure, because we are all different. I tend to spend more time training and helping a person with how to take charge of how they feel. Depression, for example, is not necessarily a person thinking negatively all the time (although it can start from there), but it slowly becomes an emotional and mental state. It becomes your automatic state and when you experience or look at something you will view it through the eyes of depression. It becomes your mindset over time.

When we go through a difficult or upsetting time or event, we react to it emotionally. How we think about the situation causes an emotional reaction. These negative emotions will sometimes show up physically. Sometimes when we are upset we physically cry. What started with a thought, becomes an emotion, and manifests physically in the body. Or a person who is anxious in their thoughts will have physical feelings of anxiety in the body, even physical symptoms of IBS, headaches or loss of appetite.

When you keep an emotional reaction going for an extended period, over time you are memorising and learning to be in that state. You are making a habit of how you feel. This impacts what you believe about yourself and your situation and, as a result, your identity. As this diagram demonstrates, when we are governed by how we feel, it controls everything:

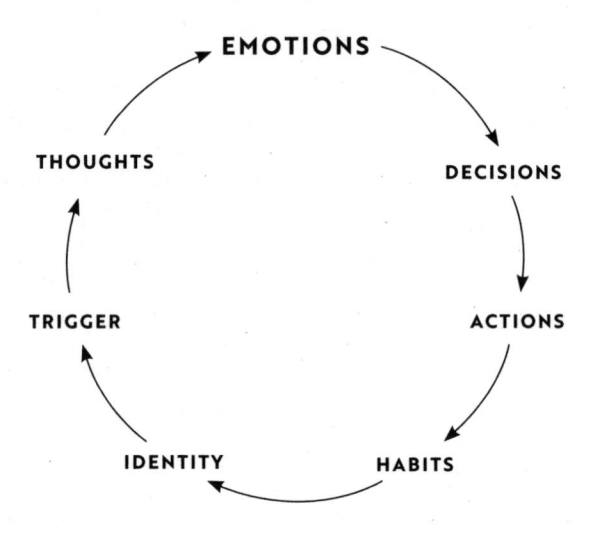

EMOTIONS → DECISIONS → ACTIONS → HABITS → IDENTITY → TRIGGER → THOUGHTS → EMOTIONS

Good news

If your mind and body can work together to reinforce a negative state, then you can use this same mechanism to reinforce a positive state that serves you better. You can break a negative emotional reaction by taking action to do something that generates a more positive emotional reaction.

I must add at this point that getting yourself checked out by your doctor is so important. Deficiencies in our minerals or vitamins can also have an impact on our state. Regardless of cause, what I share in the next few chapters will help you feel better when put into practise.

Your feelings are valid

Your emotions tell you a lot about how you are processing things. As such, emotions are always valid. I've had clients feel angry at themselves for being upset. Allow yourself to feel what you feel and don't try to suppress the emotions. Suppressing only leads to more problems down the road. Speaking with a trusted friend, partner or professional is sometimes needed to vent about how we are feeling. Emotions are valid, even when we don't want to feel that way. It is healthy to accept how you feel and then work towards changing the emotions if you feel they are not serving you well. You can't choose what you feel all the time. You can influence how you feel, and you can choose how you react to how you feel. The start of changing your emotional state starts with processing emotions and taking responsibility for how you respond. Don't be in denial about how you feel; instead, accept that how you feel is an indication that something isn't right for you.

The light switch in the darkness

Imagine standing in the middle of a dark room, where you can't see anything. However, the light switch is there. Light exists, even if it's not shining right now. If happiness is the light bulb and sadness is the darkness, then the only way to illuminate the light is to press the switch. To escape this darkness, we first need to find the switch. This is how it can be at first when you know you want to be happy again, but all you see is darkness. When a person feels like everything has gone dark, my job is to help them find the switch. Emotions are very strong and shifting them is not an overnight task. It takes time.

It may feel futile at first, stumbling and tripping in the dark as you try to make a change but still not finding the light switch, taking steps but unsure what lies before you. It can be disheartening, and make us question if there's even a switch or light at all. The darkness of depression can be overwhelming, making us lose hope and motivation. But we must remember that there is a way out – we just have to take small, gradual steps.

The switch is often used to describe moments of breakthrough, a flicker of clarity or a reignited inner spark. It represents the light of life coming back on, the feeling of joy returning after battling against powerful negative emotions. People who have experienced this describe it as a renewed sense of purpose and an emergence of emotions.

CHRISTINE'S WEIGHT LOSS STORY

I got an email from a woman named Christine, who was struggling with her weight and issues around food. She was in a state of despair, feeling depressed every time she looked in a mirror. She was feeling scared that there was no hope. How would she ever be happy and have the life she always thought she would have? She felt it was too late and that the weight was too much.

Afraid of never being happy

Sometimes people actually fear feeling certain emotions due to the fact they know how debilitating they can be. Fear of being sad and unhappy, for example, can be quite overwhelming for many individuals. It often stems from a lack of awareness that you can actively work to keep yourself from having an unhappy life. Sometimes people fear being single because that would make them so unhappy and they fear this unhappy life so it results in inner anxiety. This mindset fixates on the emotional result of being single late into life and fails to see that if we want to find someone we can, but it will take decisions and actions. It all boils down to the meaning you attach to certain outcomes because the wrong meanings can cause us to get stuck. What does it mean to you if you don't achieve something you want, like getting married, having children, or securing a particular job? You might fear that if you don't achieve that 'thing', you will become depressed. This limiting belief creates a state of fear and despair. This state controls what you do and it is like having a 'why' based in fear.

You can also get caught comparing yourself to others – because you aren't at the same place in life that they are, you feel that you have missed the boat. This comparison results in feeling you failed and are subpar, so you struggle to believe that you will ever be as happy as they are. You take on the mindset that you are losing in life compared to others.

The significance you give to these events and timelines shapes your emotional responses. By exploring alternative, healthier meanings and taking time to reframe your perspectives, you can find a path that leads to contentment, even if your deepest desires remain unfulfilled. Remember, your happiness and emotional well-being are within your control, and they aren't solely reliant on external circumstances.

A significant fear people have that doesn't get talked about enough is the fear of being sad. Let's use Christine's story to explain it.

Christine felt that due to her weight she was not pretty, which resulted in her not meeting a partner, which resulted in her being lonely. The thoughts of her being lonely filled her with an image of being an old lady with lots of cats that nobody ever visited and having nobody to talk to. To her, this was a depressing image and filled her with sadness. So you could say at the end of it all, her 'what if' story resulted in sadness. She feared this sadness so much that her current joy was extinguished. She was 35 but already was visualising herself as an 85-year-old lonely woman, and her emotional state was as if she was already in that lonely situation. She projected herself into this imagined future state of loneliness and despair as if it was a matter of fact.

Nothing has meaning, except the meaning you give it

The story or meaning you believe can be seen in different ways. Your view is not the only perspective. The fact is, you have power to discourage negative emotions from within. You can stop negative emotions like depression and be content even if you don't get whatever is your heart's desire. It all comes down to the meaning. What does it mean for you if you don't achieve that thing, like getting married, having kids, getting the job? You can fill in the blank with whatever it is that you desire.

The meaning you have was created by you, therefore it can be changed by you.

It sounds impossible to think that we can be happy even if we don't get the one thing we have always desired, but it is not. It is not just changing your existing thoughts for something nice and fluffy, it needs to be a deep-down revelation of the new meaning that you feel on an emotional level. For Christine, she believed that how she looked would result in a life of sadness. We needed to find Christine's switch. I often see the switch as literally a toggle between states. Put simply: light and dark. I use this analogy because you can ask yourself the question I asked at the beginning of the chapter. What is the emotional state you are stuck in most frequently? And what is the opposite state that you would like to feel? For Christine, feeling sad was the state currently but the opposite was to be happy again.

A key question

I asked Christine a question that would be fundamental in her recovery. It's a question that I encourage everyone to ask themselves once in a while just to check in with yourself: 'When was the last time you really laughed?'

Her body language slightly changed as she recounted one particular evening when she laughed so hard with friends, she had to run to the bathroom for fear of there being an accident through tears of laughter. I ask the question as it serves as a reminder of what happiness felt like when the light used to shine brightly. It was a way to remind Christine that firstly, she still had what it took to be happy and secondly, this was the state of joy she was longing to feel again – I could see it in her as she smiled, recalling the stories of laughs and happy moments.

But if you answer with 'I can't remember the last time' or 'I don't know', it isn't necessarily a sign that you are depressed, but maybe a sign you need to laugh more. As adults we tend to get so serious with ourselves. We need to make sure we are having those moments to laugh or sing or simply have fun in life. These moments help keep you grounded and balanced not just emotionally, but biologically too, as the hormones being released from laughter or having fun also make a physical difference.

Low self-esteem can lead to low mood, even depression. That state slowly erodes our sense of self-worth further, even making us feel that we have no purpose, which costs us our motivation and drive. The good news is that those essential parts like self-worth, purpose, drive, even joy are still within us; we just need to rediscover them, just like finding a switch in a dark room. By recalling her moments of laughter it reminded Christine how it felt. This is not a cure, but a step in shifting mindset.

WHAT IS YOUR EMOTIONAL INTELLIGENCE?

We just accept being happy and never think about it. But the thing is, we should learn about what makes us happy, or at the very least what makes us less sad in a situation. Emotional intelligence means understanding what makes us feel a certain way.

Emotional intelligence is also known as emotional quotient or EQ. It is the ability to be aware of how you feel and having the awareness to manage your feelings in a positive way. Being self-aware and knowing when to relieve stress, how to communicate effectively, empathising with others and how to defuse conflict – all require a level of emotional intelligence. This self-awareness can be learned over time and it can be life changing when we get to grips with how we process things. It is one of the elements I teach in my monthly coaching group; it always gets a great reaction because for many it is not something that they've heard before.

WHAT DEPRESSION SHOWS YOU

Depression has shown me how powerful an emotional state can be. It has the power to stop a person and cause them to lose all hope. It can cause a person to not want to get out of bed, to give up on a dream, or in the worst cases, cause a human being to want to stop going on with life. Emotions are powerful. Look at anger for example. It can cause people to kill another human. The perpetrator knows their freedom will be taken away forever but in the heat of anger their reason is completely gone. Emotions, when strong enough, can control us. There is a lesson in that. If negative emotions can control you and cause you to do things you would never have thought of doing, then isn't the same true for positive ones? How powerful are love, joy and hope? If emotions have the power to control us negatively then it must be true that they can also influence us positively. That is the power of emotions.

The inner power station

Think of yourself like a power station. The power you create is either positive or negative – the power being our emotions turn on the light or turn it off. From this station, the power will always be generated whether you are self-aware or not. The point is that we are always generating emotions, just like you are always thinking consciously and subconsciously.

That being said, you tend not to consciously make decisions to do things that will help you generate the right type of emotions. Your main focus isn't always your emotional and mental well-being. However, if this process is always happening, shouldn't you be taking some charge of it? Of course, the answer is yes, but the big problem is you tend to leave it at the bottom of your list until you start to feel off and by then the lifestyle you have created doesn't facilitate much of anything that helps you mentally or emotionally. It has gone too far and it won't just shift overnight. Depression or bitterness, for example, are states that are slow to come on you and slow to shake. Fleeting anger can be fast to come on and fast to dissipate, but real anger can be years in the making until it eventually erupts.

You can influence the emotional power station to produce positive emotions if you take action. It won't be overnight, but in time your consistent effort will take effect. That is the hardest part for many: taking action without seeing immediate results, trying to find the switch in the dark.

We are a fast-paced generation that like things to happen instantly. But it is a misconception that everything needs to be instant to be worthwhile. As we all have probably experienced in life, things that are of value take time. Like trying to run 10 kilometres. If you've never done it then you are going to struggle on the first kilometre, but over time you add in a few more metres until eventually you can make the 10k.

We attach meanings to things all the time. It is how we learn and grow as a person. For example, the universal common meaning of fire goes like this. We learn by experience that if we touch the fire or something hot it will hurt. Hot things mean danger. On the other hand, certain days have more meaning in them than others to some people because of culture or religion. For some people, Christmas is a very important date in the diary filled with love and joy, for others it is the remembrance of the birth of Jesus Christ, for still others it is a reminder of how their loved ones aren't around anymore and it is filled with sadness and feeling lonely. But then for lots of people it is just another day with no real meaning at all because in their culture it isn't celebrated. The same thing can have different meanings associated with it for different people.

EXERCISE
SLOWLY AND STEADILY BUILDS THINGS OF STRENGTH

For Christine, progress was slow and steady over a few sessions, but the result she achieved of overcoming her fear of being lonely was just brilliant. Here is a brief synopsis of how Christine got out of feeling emotionally stuck in a state of sadness and low self-esteem. This exercise shows the prompts that you can apply to your situation of emotional entanglement.

> **Changing how we feel about something means changing the meaning we gave it.**

Step one: evaluate how you mostly feel in a week

In the feelings log to follow I need you to fill it in as you go, or at the end of the day, by marking which emotions you felt in that day that you remember. Go through the list each time and tick what you felt. We aren't always aware of the many emotions we can feel, and this list is to show you that we aren't just happy or sad or angry. There are so many more ways to describe how we feel and this is a great tool for becoming emotionally self-aware. Journalling like this is simple but eye opening.

Here are a few of the most well-researched benefits of writing down how you feel:

- **INCREASED FOCUS AND CONCENTRATION:** Writing can help you to focus and concentrate on the task at hand without feeling the emotions as strongly as you would when thinking about the problem. When you are writing, you are forced to slow down and think about what you are doing.
- **BETTER PROBLEM-SOLVING SKILLS**: Writing down your thoughts helps you to see them more clearly and to organise them in a logical way. This can help you to identify the root of the problem and to develop a solution.
- **INCREASED CREATIVITY:** Writing things down can help you to be more creative in finding solutions.
- **REDUCED STRESS:** When you write about your thoughts and feelings, you are able to process them and to let go of them. This can help you to feel calmer and more in control.

I asked Christine to express how she was feeling and why. Over time we looked at what meaning she had associated with being overweight, looking at the identity she was seeing for herself. Here is a feelings log to give you a way to monitor your emotional site overtime. This gave us a way to monitor what emotions were most dominant.

	MONDAY	TUESDAY	WEDNESDAY	THURSDAY	FRIDAY	SATURDAY	SUNDAY
HAPPY							
SAD							
EXCITED							
ANGRY							
IRRITATED							
FRUSTRATED							
PROUD							
REGRETFUL							
DISGUSTED							
MOTIVATED							
GUILTY							
ASHAMED							
ANXIOUS							
CONFIDENT							
RESENTFUL							
GLOOMY							
FEARFUL							
SCARED							
PANICKED							
GRATEFUL							
UNMOTIVATED							
PEACEFUL							

Step two: recall

Recalling happier moments shows us that it is possible to change our emotional state through memory and visualisation. This acts as evidence that we can influence the emotions we generate even if it is only for a moment.

    I asked Christine to recall happier times and fond memories to stir up those more positive emotions from memory. This is not a cure: it is a reminder that happiness is possible because sometimes people feel they've lost the ability to be happy. Recalling these fond stories is a way to show that they can feel again. Remember the power plant. I was helping her to recall happier times to generate a tiny bit of positive emotional state to prove she was capable and remind her how it feels.

Step three: new meaning

Take a moment to explore why the emotion you have observed in your feelings log is regularly showing up. What is the meaning you have assigned to it, and what can you do to change the meaning.

> **You cannot change the past, but you can change how you view it in the present.**

The goal is not to make you happy about a sad situation that may have happened to you. What I want you to see is that the meanings we assign may be just as painful as the event itself. Look at your situation and get professional help if you struggle to change the meaning. Sometimes it is hard to grasp another meaning when we are stuck in an existing one.

We created new meaning for Christine. This is a synopsis of how we constructed healthier, accurate meanings:

LIMITING BELIEF: *Being overweight makes me undesirable and will lead to a lonely, sad life. Loneliness is my fear.*
NEW BELIEF: We explored how being alone is not automatically linked to depression because there are people who like being on their own and who are not depressed. Loneliness due to wanting a partner was what she feared. That led us to the next part.

We explored the reality that if she didn't want to be alone, she didn't have to be. Granted, she couldn't make someone love her, but marriage was not the only solution to loneliness. There are other ways like having friends, clubs, hobbies with others, and so on. This gave Christine back a sense that she had control whether she was lonely or not.

LIMITING BELIEF: *I am undesirable due to my weight.*
NEW BELIEF: If your weight was indicative of how desirable you were then only slim people would be happily married, which is simply false, proving that her belief was false.

The new belief was that loving oneself is key and this made her desirable, as studies show.

We explored how she viewed herself and we developed a healthier identity for her to pursue – one that emphasised being content and loving the skin she was in. Previously, whenever she had tried to lose weight, she was motivated by the fear of being alone and it was not lasting. However, now she was motivated by loving who she was and the person she saw herself becoming. Her new identity led to her becoming healthier for herself and how she saw her future self. Christine found this new motivation and love for the outdoors and built a whole plan around physical challenges she wanted to achieve. She was now living life true to herself, not her fears. We did a lot of self-development work on top of this and she became crystal clear on her identity.

LIMITING BELIEF: *I can't make someone love me.*

NEW BELIEF: This belief caused her such panic at times when she used to think about it, but now she knew that she was in control of her feelings. Christine now knew that she could control how she felt every day by what she did and how she spent her time. Loneliness was a state of mind, and she had the power to have other methods of filling the void if she ever felt like that. She also now knew that when she loved herself and life, she was most desirable.

Step four: action

Christine's progress was not just about the new meaning and beliefs – it was also important to exercise and do things that would physically help her feel a little better – things that generate feel-good hormones such as dopamine, serotonin, endorphins and oxytocin. You can boost levels of these hormones with some simple lifestyle changes, like diet, exercise and expressing gratitude, and subsequently improve your mood.

Setting out a plan of action is not about filling a whole day with tasks and challenges. Instead, it is a plan of small baby steps you can do on a daily basis. Christine planned to walk 30 minutes a day, not to lose weight but to get moving again. The old her wanted to sit in and do nothing. But this didn't align with her true self or her values. Her new self knew she had to get moving because that is what she used to love doing, simply walking. She was aligning her actions with her true self. The story or meaning we are playing for ourselves is so important because this is what we live by. Our beliefs and values are our identity. When we don't live in a way that is true to ourselves, we become disjointed and unhappiness sets in.

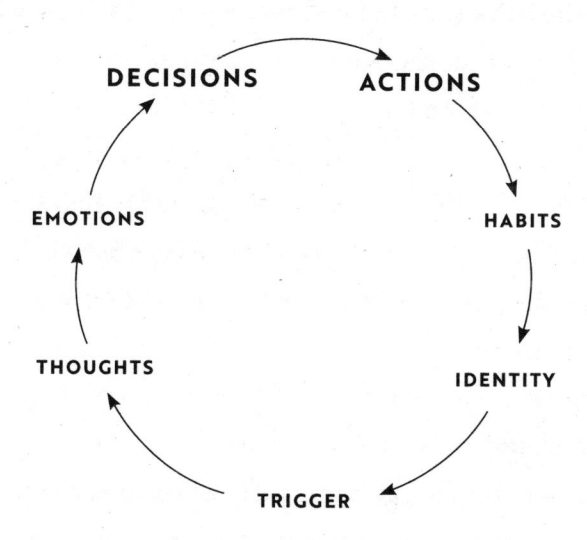

DECISIONS → ACTIONS → HABITS → IDENTITY → TRIGGER → THOUGHTS → EMOTIONS → DECISIONS

Do what you have to do in spite of how you feel. Do what aligns with the person you see yourself becoming. Your thoughts and feelings may be screaming at you to just go back to bed. But the real key is trusting. Trusting the process with the hope that it will bring change. You don't feel like doing it, you may struggle to focus your thoughts on doing it, but you need to do it, and not think. Changing the meaning is the start of healing.

Step five: monitor

Monitoring yourself helps keep you from slipping backwards and also helps you to see improvement, which inevitably will spur you on.

Over time Christine continued to monitor her emotional state, and her emotional intelligence grew immensely. There were other limiting beliefs that showed up, but dealing with them got easier with this new identity in place. How we see ourselves is how we will be. Christine's walks became hikes. She joined hike clubs, got back her love for the outdoors and walked the Camino. Baby steps became giant leaps.

SOMETIMES IT'S WHAT YOU DO, NOT WHAT YOU THINK, THAT DEFINES YOU

We assign meanings all the time to people, places and things. Stories we create in our heads about ourselves and the world around us. Meanings are powerful because they are what we believe. But those meanings aren't always accurate or true. Meanings can be changed, and that change starts with questioning the stories we tell ourselves and challenging assigned meanings that may not serve us or reflect the reality of the situation. If you don't like how you feel, it goes back to what you are thinking, and what you are thinking is either based on a truth or a lie.

The meanings we tell ourselves are so influential in how we live our lives because it is from these meanings that we generate either positive or negative emotions. Like the person who believes they are 'not enough' or are 'unlovable' – these mindsets came from a meaning that generated emotions. If you don't like how you feel, look at why you feel that way. It might be time to change the meaning you choose to believe.

There are also other things we can do to control our mindset and how we feel both emotionally and physically; we will explore them in the next chapter. Exercise, lifestyle and social support are all important. It starts with finding the switch.

Decide who you are, don't wait to feel it.

CHAPTER 10

Physically stuck: when your body lets you down

You may be physically or biologically stuck because of tangible limitations in your body that prevent you from attaining or achieving certain things. It could be because of neurodiversity, a scar from an operation, or something irreversible like an injury that restricts your mobility. It could be a unique physical condition that sets you apart from others, or a perceived flaw in your appearance that affects your self-esteem. We may try to conceal it, but deep down, we all long to just fit in.

But is fitting in a goal we should set for ourselves? What if we made our goal to accept ourselves just as we are? Accepting ourselves and our quirks allows us to make peace with who we are as opposed to resisting it. Rather than try to fit in to be like others, set your normal based on your identity.

I have worked with countless people wanting to lose weight because they hate what they see in the mirror. But what I have discovered is that real breakthrough happens when we change our inner views of ourselves. Rather than despising how you look now, embrace it and let the energy go into changing what you dislike rather than wasting time in the spiral of self-hate and putting yourself down. You can't change certain things about your appearance, but the key is to get clarity on what you want and change what you can. When we have a clear objective, a plan to get us there and a loving, patient attitude towards ourselves, then weight loss can be achieved (but, most importantly, maintained).

Sometimes, physical limitations are thrust upon us abruptly, through accidents or injuries that alter our abilities in an instant. Other times, we are born with these limitations, navigating a world that might not always accommodate our needs. In some cases, we yearn for something like parenthood, but face disappointment and medical challenges that prevent us from fulfilling that dream.

Living in a state of physical constraint can be an arduous journey, fraught with frustration, pain, and a deep sense of unhappiness. I intimately understand this struggle, as I have faced my own battles with being physically stuck. It can feel overwhelming, as if you are trapped in a never-ending cycle of longing and despair. But even in the face of such challenges, it is crucial to remember that our worth and potential extend far beyond our physical limitations. Our bodies do not define us unless we allow them to. If we compare ourselves to others, it creates low self-esteem, and if we try to be like others it creates frustration. The fact is, we possess resilience, strength and inner beauty that transcend any physical constraints. It is in these qualities that we can find solace and the power to overcome. A fulfilled, happy life is not defined by how you look and your limitations.

While we may not be able to change certain aspects of our bodies, we can work towards acceptance, self-love and cultivating a mindset that focuses on our unique strengths and abilities. Seeking support from loved ones, professionals or communities that understand our experiences can also provide a valuable source of encouragement and guidance.

Remember, being physically stuck does not diminish our capacity for joy, fulfilment, and happiness. It is a reminder that our worth is not solely determined by what we can or cannot do physically. By embracing our inherent worth, celebrating our strengths and cultivating a positive mindset, we can find a path to happiness and live a meaningful life, despite the physical challenges we may face.

THE LADDER OF LIFE

I think of life as being on a ladder. Each rung has significance and represents a period of time that we spend there. Sometimes we move on to the next rung satisfied and ready to add to our life, and sometimes we move on hoping to never again think of the rung we were just on. As we discussed in chapter 1, it is crucial to draw on your inner instinct, your gut, when it comes to planning and pursuing the rungs on your ladder. Everyone's ladder is different; your image of your future self could be completely different to somebody else's. You may want to disregard some rungs that others want. You might not want to settle down and have a family, or you might not ever want to buy your own home. Whatever you feel deep inside is what you should pursue and not the template that perhaps most people work from, or society sells you. There is no shame in not wanting kids, there is no shame in not wanting to get married, there is no shame in pursuing what your heart wants even when it goes against the norm, as long as it doesn't hurt anyone else. You do you and trust your gut. When I speak of being stuck it is always in reference to *you* feeling that way because of your inner desires not being achieved. Nobody else gets to climb the rungs of your ladder, it is yours alone. Other people's opinions are fine, but you get to decide whether you agree with them or not.

Maybe you feel physically stuck in the wrong job because the only reason you are there is that your parents 'strongly encouraged' you to study that degree. Or trying to find that special someone to settle down with, all you seem to be attracting is the very type that just isn't for you. You've heard the saying 'there are plenty more fish in the sea' a million times but inside you think that maybe in your life you only have a pond to work with.

Or you found that special someone, got married and now you want to have a family of your own. No matter what you do you can't make a baby appear. How do you deal with a situation that is biologically and physically out of your control? How do you cope when your dream is being slowly and painfully deconstructed before your eyes?

Physically stuck comes in many forms. Let me share my experience with you.

OUR STORY

My wife, Fiona, and I had reached a point in our lives where we had a stable home and successful businesses. The topic of children finally came up in our conversations. It was a serious discussion we had never had before, but we both felt ready and excited about the prospect of starting a family. We both love kids, and I knew Fiona would undoubtedly be an incredible, fun-loving mother, so we embarked on this journey with anticipation and excitement.

As the months went by, our initial excitement turned into disappointment, but we remained hopeful. One month of trying turned into two, six months into twelve. A year had passed. We became meticulously focused on timing everything perfectly, hoping to bring forth the bundle of joy we longed for. Along the way, friends and family started asking the dreaded question: 'So, when are you guys going to have kids?'

I found this question incredibly challenging to handle. It seemed to carry with it not only curiosity but also expectations and judgements. Even if nobody asked the question directly, I could sense it lingering in the air. It felt like the default question to ask any newly married couple. However, I wrestled with the weight it carried because it added pressure and made me feel like everyone was constantly thinking about our reproductive plans.

It's insensitive to enquire about someone's plans for having children. Nobody intentionally is trying to hurt or offend you by asking it of course, but what people may not realise is it can be a trigger for those facing difficulties in conceiving, and it really should be viewed by all as a private intimate matter. If the couple doesn't mention it, maybe it's for a reason, so don't ask even if it is coming from a good place. Be sensitive.

I've witnessed couples who, due to the fear of being asked about their attempts to conceive, start avoiding social gatherings altogether. They withdraw from friends and family to process their pain privately and shield themselves from becoming the centre of conversation. When a couple has been trying to have a child for an extended period without success, the emotional and mental toll can be overwhelming. Talking about it over casual drinks or during dinner parties becomes emotionally draining and reopens the wounds they are desperately trying to heal.

Don't get me wrong, conversation and support are crucial for those facing fertility challenges (or whatever physical situation has you feeling stuck). However, it's crucial to choose the right time and the right people to confide in. Opening up to trusted friends or seeking guidance from professionals who specialise in this area can provide the empathy and understanding that couples need. Let's be mindful of the emotional journey that others might be going through and offer our support in ways that respect their boundaries and individual processes. Just like a rung on the ladder, we can find ourselves perhaps stuck at one of these impasses in life.

The hardest part was my Fiona

We decided to see our doctor and he sent us to a fertility clinic. I vividly recall sitting in the fertility doctor's office. It was during this appointment that the doctor mentioned that tests and investigations would hopefully determine the underlying issue, potentially uncovering which one of us was the cause. This was the beginning of a long road. The mere thought that this journey, already fraught with difficulties, could reveal that one of us was responsible for our struggles was devastating. The unhelpful notion of fault became a heavy burden to carry. How could I bear the knowledge that I might be the reason that my wife's cherished dreams of motherhood remained unfulfilled? The weight of responsibility for denying my maternal, loving wife the joy of having a child was unbearable to comprehend.

It was in that moment, as the reality sunk in, that I experienced the most profound depths of sadness and despair. When your feelings of being stuck solely impact you, it's challenging enough. However, when your circumstances directly impact the person you hold dearest in the world, the magnitude of the situation intensifies exponentially. The thought of being the cause of my wife's inability to have a child, something she so deeply desired, was shattering.

We had never broached this subject before. The weight of unspoken fears and uncertainties hung heavily between us. If it turned out to be my fault, what would it mean for our relationship? How would it affect the foundation of love and support we had built together? These questions loomed large, casting a shadow over our future as a couple. We started the rounds of tests, but I needed to speak about this heavy burden.

In moments like these, it becomes clear that the emotional impact of feeling stuck extends far beyond our own individual experiences. It permeates our relationships and tests our resilience. It forces us to confront the unimaginable and navigate uncharted territories together. While the road ahead may be filled with uncertainty, I knew deep down that we would face it hand in hand, drawing strength from the bond we had forged.

Little did I know then that our journey would eventually reveal unforeseen paths and offer unexpected possibilities. It would teach us the true meaning of resilience and love, and the power of unwavering support. But in that moment, all I could do was brace myself for the unknown and hope that our shared love would carry us through the darkest of times.

Maybe you've been given a diagnosis and it impacts not just you but loved ones. Or you have a physical challenge that most don't know about, but now that you've fallen in love you know it's time to share it with your partner as it possibly impacts their future too. Maybe it's time for that conversation. I know how that goes.

The conversation

We sat down and I remember thinking to myself prior to starting the chat, what if it was the other way around, what if we couldn't have kids because of Fiona? My instinct, my gut, my true self answered this question in a nanosecond. I remember getting this almost visceral feeling of a statement that came out of nowhere: 'Fiona being happy is more important than me being happy.' I would make sure that she knew that if it was her body that was the reason for not having a child, I'd see it the same as if it was my body. We are one, so her pain is my pain, her joy is my joy, and we would face this as a team, not as individuals. I just hoped that she would see it the same way as I did.

We had the chat and one of the first things Fiona said was: 'It doesn't matter whose body is to blame, we deal with this as a couple.' I felt such relief that she saw it like I did.

In a relationship it is we not me.

In that pivotal moment, we realised that neither of us was interested in assigning blame. Instead, we chose to focus on what we could control – the health and quality of our relationship.

When it comes to challenges facing couples, life's heaviest struggles have the power to either break the couple or forge an unbreakable bond.

We embarked on a journey of growth, nurturing our relationship as the bedrock for navigating the uncertain path ahead. There were years of tests, failed attempts and some heartbreaking moments. We supported and communicated with each other on a new, profound level. Our shared burdens became the fuel for building a stronger bond. Our friends and family rallied around us, deepening our connections and creating a network of unwavering support.

In the face of adversity, we discovered the power of resilience and the strength of love. While we couldn't control the outcome, we controlled our response. This became the cornerstone of our journey – a testament to the indomitable spirit that emerges when we face life's challenges together. Love is the ultimate superpower. Sometimes having just one person who loves us can carry us through our toughest moments.

A lesson I learned

I learned the importance of not only giving time to how I felt but also time to how others may be feeling. When we take the focus off ourselves and onto others we tend to worry less and not get so depressed about things. We mustn't neglect ourselves of course, but when we focus on others and how they are doing we become less inwardly focused.

This was huge for me in dealing with our fertility issues. If I felt I was going down a rabbit hole of asking 'why me', I would stop myself and say, 'It's not just me, it's us.' This would force me to check in on Fiona and get the limelight off myself. Of course, my feelings are also valid and there were times when we would speak about how I was feeling as well as how she was feeling, but I found it so helpful to stop myself from falling into the abyss of despair by focusing on what could I do to help Fiona. Not just checking in with her and asking her how she was, but also getting her little treats or planning fun stuff, or doing things that had nothing to do with trying for a baby in order to keep spirits high and keep us tight.

But for me I realised I couldn't let it stop there. When I was speaking with clients on a one-to-one basis about their issues, I never thought of my own. Coaching was this automatic natural distraction. Helping others was clearly a great way to distract myself from my own problems. I want to note that you can't and shouldn't distract yourself all the time, because you do need to process how you feel and give it time. But limit the time you give it. Talk about your problem but don't set up camp there.

PDF: PHYSICAL – DIALOGUE – FOCUS

I don't advise aiming to distract yourself all the time in order to feel great again, because that doesn't work. No, what I learned is to give time to yourself and how you feel but also give time to how others may be feeling. Not all one way or the other, but both. Then if you are still feeling low, talk to yourself or someone you trust. Process how and why you're feeling as you do and when ready, move forward and refocus. I discovered and personally practised what became the tool that I call Physical – Dialogue – Focus, or PDF. This is a great tool for whenever you feel or think a certain way that you want to change. It is like a balm for a mental graze. When I found myself drifting into thoughts about why we couldn't have a baby, or if I felt down for whatever reason, I would use this tool. It was also a great tool for anxiety, and is something we can all practice when needed.

You remember from the previous chapters that there is a sequence to how we feel and who we become. It is:

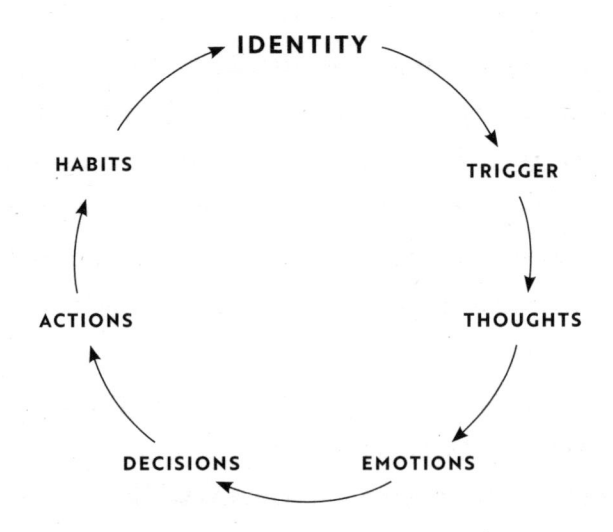

IDENTITY → TRIGGER → THOUGHTS → EMOTIONS → DECISIONS → ACTIONS → HABITS → IDENTITY

When we are triggered, and we know that thoughts around a particular issue will have a negative impact on our emotions, PDF can be inserted. It goes something like this:

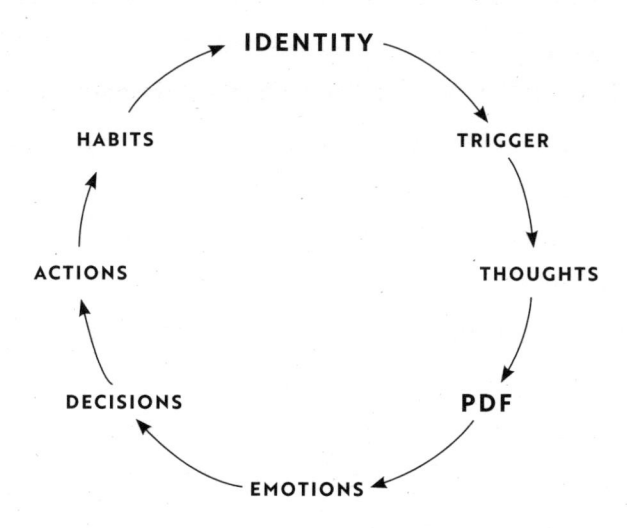

```
        IDENTITY
   HABITS      TRIGGER
   ACTIONS     THOUGHTS
   DECISIONS   PDF
        EMOTIONS
```

Knowing where it goes is key, but you can use this tool at any point along the sequence. The sooner you use it the better and more effective it will be. Even using it later in the sequence is better than never. We have looked at other tools that break the sequence in earlier chapters; these can also be used, however they do require you to take time out to work through. PDF, on the other hand, is an instant tool that we can practise in conjunction with the other tools.

For many people who are in the situation of not being able to conceive, they feel something like grief. There is a sense of loss that the child you always imagined having and raising is being taken away from you; the lost experiences, the lost memories that you hoped would be created as the years raising the child played out.

The inherent maternal/paternal gene that many of us have that makes us want to raise a family can also give a sense of purpose, even duty. You work hard to get to a place in life where you can have and support a child, but now that is not going to be your path.

I needed a tool to deal with this and that's where PDF helped a lot. I needed an intervention when the thoughts would try to spiral to a place of gloom – a way to know and reassure myself that I can be happy even when things don't work out. I needed a way to stop the negative spiral of thoughts and stop myself from going down a road of grief and sadness. PDF was like first aid for me.

We've all experienced those moments when our attention gets interrupted by a ringing phone or a notification from social media. In an instant, our thoughts scatter and our attention is diverted.

But here's the thing: these interruptions are not just limited to our devices. They can also occur within our minds. Negative thoughts or triggers can pop up unexpectedly, derailing our mental focus and dragging us into a spiral of emotions.

Here's what can help: recognising that just like we can put our phones on silent or adjust our notifications, we also have the power to silence those negative thoughts and regain our mental focus. We can choose to redirect our attention back to the task at hand and let go of those distractions. It takes practice, but with time and awareness, we can cultivate the ability to acknowledge and let go of negative thoughts and triggers.

So, the next time your mind gets interrupted by a negative thought, remember that you have the power to regain control. Just like adjusting your phone settings or closing unnecessary tabs, you can refocus your mind and continue with clarity and purpose.

Side note: I must stress that I used PDF after time had passed and I had made sense of how I was feeling. PDF was a tool to use because I had had enough of the negative thoughts and there wasn't much more to process, that work had been done (as discussed in previous chapters). However, there will always be new variations or new triggers that would show up so it wasn't as if I could always take time to get processing all those thoughts. I would take note of them, even write them into my phone like a journal, so that I could later, at a time that suited, get to making sense of them. These negative thoughts are so powerful they can distort your whole day if allowed. I would take note of any constant thoughts or trends in my thinking and feelings and if they kept showing up I would then actually allocate a time to make sense of them.

Step one: P for physical

Studies have shown that unpredictable events, due to their unfamiliar sudden appearance, can instantly capture our attention. What's even more powerful is that physical movement can disrupt our cognitive function. When triggered, automatic thoughts arise, but at that moment, a simple physical change can be effective in diverting those thoughts. Our minds can only focus on one thing at a time, even if thoughts race quickly. So, performing a small physical action like standing up, making a cup of tea, clapping hands, leaning back in a chair, or looking out the window can interrupt the flood of negative thoughts that may have been about to consume us. Our mind can only focus on one thing at a time. It may fly between thoughts very fast, but it is still only dealing with one thing at a time. A simple physical movement or even a verbal 'okay, that's that' or putting on a song can help. Anything that gets you to move, no matter how little it might be, can help you interrupt the flood of negative thoughts. But we won't stop there: next we are going to process and refocus our thoughts.

MOTION CREATES EMOTION

Movement will interrupt the negative emotions that were about to flow. It doesn't stop them completely, but it slows them. How we feel originates with our thoughts, so interrupting a potential negative thought or at the very least introducing another thought helps curb their impact. Instead of your brain going all in on a negative thought, it now has to participate in movement. Any form of movement has this effect to some degree. Even if it is tiny, it is better than nothing.

Studies have also shown that people become more emotionally engaged with something when they're also physically engaged. This is powerful. Suppose for example you want to run five kilometres. You tell yourself in your mind, 'I can do this'. Now tell yourself 'I can do this' while actually running and watch how your focus will feel far greater. When you are running and trying to go for a personal best, keep that dialogue going and you'll see how focused you become. For me I had to think about how I could be happy if I don't have kids, and how we could be happy as a couple, as well as the uncertainty of going through something that nobody I knew could relate to. It felt like everyone had kids. If those thoughts came in, I would actually clap my hands once to interrupt them.

EXERCISE

Exercise is another powerful interruption to negative triggers. But it is not always achievable when you are right in the middle of work, sitting at your desk. You can't suddenly jump up and start doing burpees, star jumps or press-ups beside the desk. Instead, you can take a milder approach, for example going for a brief walk on your break or getting off the bus a stop early on the way home so you can walk for a bit. Exercise, as we know, releases all the right hormones to help us deal with stress, anxiety and tension. Simple movement alone helps get the tension out of muscles. A stretch break could also be your interruption as part of the P section. If you are in a position to exercise, it is a long-term method to help keep you less stressed. We are designed to move and our minds and bodies benefit from movement, so it helps us deal with challenges more effectively. There was a time I hated going to the gym. But when I saw how it helped me deal with stress and benefited my mood and actually gave me more energy over time, I was hooked. Of course, there are physical health benefits too, so it is a win-win. My point is, when you get stressed, triggered or otherwise, a great way to stop the spiral is to get moving.

BOX BREATHING

My personal greatest tool for interrupting a trigger or unwanted thinking is box breathing. It is a great way to control yourself and interrupt stress, anxiety, panic attacks or any other emotional/physical state that affects your calm. Box breathing is powerful at communicating to the mind and body how to feel. It is used by the Navy Seals to help them deal and cope with high stress combat situations and even torture. Here is how it works.

Get comfortable if you can. You should not feel light-headed or dizzy while doing the exercise; if you do, you must stop the exercise as it means you are not doing it correctly.

The four steps of box breathing are:
STEP ONE:
- Get into a seated position ideally (but you can do it standing, just be careful).
- Inhale slowly through your nose while mentally counting to four.
- Focus on filling your lungs and abdomen with air.
- Notice and feel how air is filling your lungs.

STEP TWO:
- Now hold that breath and mentally count to four again.

STEP THREE:
- Exhale slowly through your mouth while mentally counting to four.
- Concentrate on getting all the air out of your lungs at once.

STEP FOUR:
- Hold your breath with your lungs emptied and mentally count to four again.

Return to step one and repeat the process until you can feel yourself becoming calmer and more relaxed. If you cannot count to four, try just counting to three.

Box breathing is something that Navy Seals do for about five minutes to reduce that sense of stress, or the flight or fight response. Box breathing is sometimes referred to as tactical breathing because it assists soldiers in dealing with high-stress situations during combat and battle.

I remember a psychiatrist telling me of an old technique to break a rumination: have an elastic band on your wrist and flick it when you wanted to get yourself out of your head. Physical interruption is effective in intervening in your cognitive process in aid of stopping further ruminating.

Performing these interruptions puts you in a far stronger position to move to the next step.

Step two: D for dialogue

Inner dialogue is what we are saying to ourselves. It's not always actual words; more often than not it is a series of images or memories replayed to reinforce what we are being triggered about. For example, you might feel 'I'm no good at my job' and in that very instant, memories of how you failed before or struggled in the past come to mind. It's as if your mind is saying, 'Yes that's right, you are no good, look at all the other times you felt like this too, you're just no good.' That is why we must physically interrupt and address and process what we are saying, thinking and feeling, also known as our inner dialogue. You must have that physical interruption because it gives your thinking an opportunity to be open to an alternative. Our inner dialogue or inner narrative, as we have discussed before, is hugely influential in our state of mind and emotional state.

PROCESS

Allow yourself to process the negative thought from an observational perspective, as if watching your thoughts on a screen. Now maybe at the point in time that you are triggered, it doesn't suit, so you make a conscious decision to plan a worry time. 'I'll worry about this at 3 p.m.' But you must process it and not try push it under the rug. A note, however, that if you are dealing with an overwhelming trigger and to try processing it would mean thinking about a traumatic scenario, this is best done with a professional. I mention this because some things need to be processed in stages, and if you find that you are being triggered by something to do with a trauma, then plan a date with a professional and make the decision to wait to process until you are with them. PDF is more useful for the thoughts you can just about manage. It is the go-to after you have done the work to process your thoughts using the tools from previous chapters. When you have put plenty of time into understanding and processing how you feel and are ready to move on from it, that is when PDF comes into play. It is for when we are moving forward and dealt with and processed our troubling thoughts.

The XYZ method that we looked at in chapter 1 helps processing a lot. This time, we are going to change 'I feel' to 'I am tempted to feel'.

'I am tempted to feel X because of Y.'

This is a subtle way of identifying the thought without agreeing with the emotion. For me it was this: 'I am tempted to feel sad because of not being able to have kids.'

Fill it in yourself.

'I am tempted to feel _____ because of _____.'

It is so liberating when we start processing why we feel the way we do.

ADDRESS

Next, we address the thought or trigger with the solution. Rather than allow the negative dialogue to continue, we now present ourselves with an alternative that we would rather dwell on. This is not easy at first and it takes practice, but it is life changing when you get in the habit of it. You become your own coach and hold your mind to account. Addressing the thought could go as follows: 'I am tempted to feel _____ because of _____. But I won't because _____ and that is the truth.'

Here are some examples:

- 'I am tempted to feel unloved because of my past. But I won't because that's an old lie I used to tell myself and I know I am lovable and that is the truth.'
- 'I am tempted to feel I'm not enough because of what my teachers said. I know those thoughts are untrue because I am well able and that is the truth.'
- 'I am tempted to feel angry towards them because of what they did to me. But I won't because I've I forgiven them and they can't hurt me anymore and that is the truth.'
- 'I am tempted to feel inferior because of my diagnosis. But I won't because I am no less of a human and that is the truth.'

For me it was this: 'I am tempted to feel sad because of not being able to have children. But I won't because I am grateful for the blessings I do have and there are people in far worse positions than me and that is the truth.'

At first I spent more time on the processing part than the addressing part. But over time as I figured things out, I realised that the answers did exist, and the sentence became complete. Other triggers came along and I had to create an address for them too. I didn't always have a second part or a reply that would serve me better. But over time and with constant effort I figured them out. Like affirmations, they don't work too well unless there is complete understanding and feeling in them. You must say it because a part of you believes it with conviction. Only then do they help. I have found that the address section of the statement can be an affirmation or even a mantra you are working to believe. I've seen people use scripture and quotes as their address part.

Our inner dialogue may not have words, but instead be made up of mental images that need changing; images that get a visceral response from us when we are triggered. Whether you are dealing with words or images, or both, identify what needs changing.

Going back to the identity piece, I now began to see myself and Fiona as happy even if we couldn't have kids. I imagined what we would do that would give us joy. I saw that before we tried for children we were very happy and in reality nothing about our lives had changed. We had what we needed to be happy in other ways. Happiness was possible and that gave me hope. I would focus on the things we had that brought us joy, my identity was myself and Fiona happy. That was the target and, fast forward to today, we got there.

Think of it like this: in a court case there is an allegation by the prosecution. The defendant 'you' must then respond as to why the allegation is false. Think of the allegation as 'I am tempted to feel X because of Y'. But your response is 'I won't accept that charge because of Z and that is the truth.' You are the judge and jury, and it is up to you to decide what is your truth. We aren't putting on a trial to figure out if the negative thought is true, instead we are identifying the allegation as false and choosing to believe the truth. For the truth will set you free. For me the allegation was 'we can't be happy without kids' but the truth we chose to believe was we would be happy.

SO WHAT TO WHAT IFS

One of the greatest little dialogue edits that really helped me was when I stopped taking my thoughts so seriously. When the fear of 'what if this happens?' or 'what if that happens?' came over me, I started to say 'So what!' in response. Humour is so powerful. It wasn't that I didn't care, I just realised I am much better served in life when I don't take every thought I have so seriously. This includes horrible thoughts: I could dismiss them with a flippant 'So what'. Because if the fearful or horrible thought is in my head, then I don't take it seriously unless it is actually happening. It is acknowledging that thoughts are just that and nothing more. The anxious 'what ifs' that would run through my mind never got to take hold because the response – 'So what' – showed my mind I didn't care for the thought and so no emotional reaction occurred and the thought dissipated. My D for dialogue got to a place of saying 'So what' to what ifs. No more trying to figure out the fear

I just started to discredit anything that would cause me to feel a way I didn't want to emotionally feel.

We can believe the lie or decide on the truth, and that is what dialogue is. It is the dialogue and inner narrative that we believe is the truth. It is our response that we know is the better way to think that matters. Repeatedly working on our self-awareness leads to progress over time and we learn so much about ourselves. The truth is that we are in control of our happiness regardless of our situation. Choosing an inner narrative that will not limit us and won't take away our peace is our choice. You get to decide what the truth is for you.

Step three: F for focus

Focus is the final step in PDF. It is what follows after you respond to your inner self with the truth you chose to hold on to. You may not feel convinced of this truth just yet. It might feel foreign to tell yourself that you are enough when you've felt less than your whole life. But through breaking and intervening in the negative thought process, you will recondition yourself to align with your newfound truth that you really do matter, you are loved and you've always been enough.

Focus is the decision to get back to the task that was interrupted or to whatever you know needs to be done. Focus may also be concentrating your attention on something that keeps the intervention going. This could be something like picking up the phone to chat to a family member, popping on music, reading a book or messaging someone. The key is that it must engage you. It has to be something that you know will draw your attention. Something that is almost immersive. In a nutshell, a focus demands your attention. And a focus that engages us will keep the negative thoughts at bay. At first it might be hard because the trigger, thought or memory may still be circling in your head like a vulture circling its prey. They may come back in later, but all you need to do is keep focus.

Focus is a manual way to call attention to our mind and body and set them to work. Even if you aren't fully focused at first, stick with it and watch how it works. Again, I must stress that this works best when we have taken that moment to process and address. With the physical intervention and inner dialogue of truth coupled with the image and dialogue to reinforce it, we are ready as we tell the brain to refocus.

For me, I would focus on what I could be grateful for and practise gratitude. This worked because I had images in my head of stories and experiences that gave me perspective. I learned to focus on what I had rather than what I didn't have.

Gratitude is a powerful tool worth honing. What have you got that is worth taking stock of? We spend so much of our time and energy on the things that we are working towards. How often do we spend time and energy enjoying and embracing what we already have? If you can find just one thing to be grateful for and focus your mind on how much it blesses you, that can tip the scales towards feeling better about things.

For example, I'll never forget when I visited my grandmother in a hospice in her last days. I remember leaving the building, going out through the reception, and thinking that the people in those rooms would give anything to be able to leave this place of their own accord. They didn't get to have the simplest experiences in life like going for a coffee, seeing a sunrise, cooking a meal or even just going to the shops to have a look around. My grandmother used to say that as long as you're vertical, you have more than most, and this is so true. As long as we have breath in our lungs, we have something precious. How many people don't realise that today is their very last day of life? I would default to those images when tempted to feel low or despair.

There is so much pain and suffering in the world and I decided to focus as best I could on what really matters: the fact that I am alive. I couldn't have kids, but I was not going to let that limit me or control my life. Society shows us as we grow up what the 'perfect family' should look like and that very image puts distress in our hearts for we feel we may not achieve the status quo. But the truth is there is no perfect family, and there is certainly no one-size-fits-all answer. I realised that I don't have to have kids to be part of a family. Family looks so different to many people and can be created not just by blood relations. Family can be adoption, fostering or helping parent a child by being an uncle or aunt. Family can be created even when people aren't biologically related. Friends can be like family. Fiona and I are a family, along with all our other relatives. I became grateful for what I do have, and I do what I can to enjoy this gift called life and those I love. Eventually I got this to flow through my mind whenever I got triggered and it became my focus, it was my truth and my identity. Then it became automatic to the extent that the trigger became less and less powerful. This way of thinking became my reality and still is to this day.

I even consider how not having kids has allowed me help so many more people with my coaching. I have time for speaking at companies, colleges and schools. If I had kids, I couldn't do half what I do, so I've made peace with the fact this is how things are meant to be. Once again, it's *amor fati* or 'love of fate'.

Accept your journey, survive your journey and find what you can love and be grateful for.

This is how you create a focus that inspires you rather than discourages you. No matter how dark life gets, or how difficult challenges may be, there is always something we can find to be grateful for. It is that thing we cling to and focus on.

The PDF is something we grow into over time. It is done alongside the techniques in the previous chapters of this book. We need to unbox what we fear and get to grips with what actually is holding us back and causing distress. Eventually I got to a place where I was fully at peace but I had processed things enough that all I now needed was the PDF technique to keep me on track.

EXERCISE
CREATE YOUR PDF SEQUENCE

Create the PDF sequence for yourself and memorise it. At first it will be hard to establish this new response but in time, through repetition, it will begin to stick. Consistency will get you there.

P: Start practising changing your physical state. Remember, simple physical change in position is all that's needed, it's an interruption however minor.

D: Take note of what inner dialogue you need to change and also of new narratives so you can recall them in a moment. In time they will become instinctive responses. Notice what works for you and keep a little journal to record it. This is what you value: your truth, your identity.

F: Make a decision to engage with something. It could be a task you were just working on, writing an email or going for a walk with music on. In other words, completely shift to something that consumes you. The key is to find something that is mentally engaging, leaving little room to think of anything else. Mindfully decide, 'Right I am doing this now' and go do it there and then.

ACCEPTING WHAT IS BEYOND OUR CONTROL

After undergoing all the tests, Fiona and I discovered that we both tested perfectly. So who or what was to blame for our inability to conceive? The diagnosis we received was 'unexplained infertility'. Years of trying fertility treatments, procedures and options and of numerous fertility doctors, left us exhausted. We don't have our own biological children.

Some things are simply beyond our physical control, yet that doesn't limit us entirely. We may not be able to fly on our own, but we can certainly catch a flight and explore the world. Someone who has lost a limb cannot magically grow a new one, but they can adapt and make modifications to their living environment.

You might have a diagnosis or disability, but you can still have a life that is full. No matter the situation, there is always something we can do.

We can redirect our focus to other areas of life and enhance them. In my case, my coaching career flourished because I had a new passion and understanding for when we are physically challenged. I also had more time available that child-rearing responsibilities would have otherwise demanded. Our marriage grew stronger, and we found joy in supporting and nurturing the children in our extended family, such as nieces, nephews, and godchildren. Mother Teresa, one of the most renowned and impactful mothers in history, didn't have any biological children of her own, yet she touched the lives of thousands, if not millions.

Even if you can't have biological children, you can still experience the profound joys of parenthood through various avenues. Whatever your physical challenge may be, don't allow it to hinder your ability to live a fulfilled life. You don't have to let it define you or hold you back.

Fiona and I have learned that happiness is still attainable, a full life is achievable even when things don't go according to plan. Embrace the concept of *amor fati*, and continue living fully, embracing all that life has to offer. Disability or inability should never define you.

You define your truth, you define who you are.

CHAPTER 11
Relationally stuck: love and sex

REPAIRING HEARTBREAK

There are a few different ways that you might become relationally stuck. It could be the fact you are single but desire to have a relationship. It could be that you are stuck in a relationship that is toxic. It could also be from heartbreak. (In the next chapter we will look at platonic interpersonal relationships with acquaintances, friends and family. This chapter, however, focuses on romantic relationships.)

Life can be incredibly unfair, especially when it comes to relationships. Someone you care for deeply and trust completely can unexpectedly turn around and hurt you. The only way to protect yourself from being hurt by others is to avoid forming close bonds altogether. I recall a girl I coached who, after experiencing multiple heartbreaks and failed relationships, watched the movie *Castaway* starring Tom Hanks. She thought to herself, 'If I lived on an island, my heart could never be broken again.' Her heart had been broken so many times in the past, even in seemingly healthy relationships. But is becoming a recluse truly the answer?

Many people choose that path, not necessarily living on a literal island, but mentally isolating themselves from those around them. They withdraw from the world, spending their lives guarded and shielded, in an attempt to protect their hearts from further pain.

In this chapter, we explore the pain of heartbreak and the breaking of trust. We discuss what to do when you find yourself stuck in a toxic relationship, when the end of a relationship leaves you feeling trapped or when it might be better to be on your own. We also address the situation where you have closed yourself off from others, becoming hardened and untrusting.

Cocaine and a heartbreak

The Cocaine and a Heartbreak Study was conducted by neuroscientist Lucy Brown, a clinical professor of neurology at Albert Einstein College of Medicine in the Bronx, New York.[5] A study of the brain was done with participants who had been through a recent heartbreak. To qualify, participants had to have been the one on the receiving end of a rejection. They were asked to bring a photo of the person with them and sit in a brain scanner. While looking at the photo, activity in the brain was observed. The results were so shocking that the study became quite infamous.

There was actual neurophysiological activity when the participant was looking at the photograph while in the brain scanner. This proved that heartbreak triggers our brain activity. Heartbreak is felt on a physical, visceral level and can be seen in the brain, so it is no wonder that break ups affect us so badly when the love was strong.

Comparisons were then carried out to see what else caused this level of brain activity so that a reference could be established. Different comparisons were made and the one that was most similar (and surprising) was of an addict withdrawing from cocaine. It turned out that addicts who went cold turkey from drugs experienced the same neurophysiological activity as people who had recently been rejected. The similarities were uncanny. The withdrawal of someone's love leads to similar brain activity and reaction as someone withdrawing from cocaine or an opioid.

We can explain so much by knowing this result. When we are rejected and the person withdraws their love we are left with a void, an emptiness, just like an addict having their drug removed. We are physically, emotionally and mentally affected by the breakup.

This heartbreak is so painful and hurtful because when the love we once received from someone is removed, we are left in a state of pain, and the antidote is in the hands of the person who caused the pain. This is why a person might go on the rebound, trying to get the fix from someone willing to give it and who somewhat fits the qualities of their last partner. We actually experience 'love withdrawal', as I call it. We crave that person who rejected us. Whether it was the perfect relationship or a bad one – even if the relationship was toxic at times or they didn't treat us right – we crave the love that is now gone. And it is not just a partner who can break our heart; a parent, child, sibling or friend can also leave us with that heartache.

Obsessed with 'Why me?'

Then there is the obsessing about why it didn't work out. What did they mean when they said 'It's me, not you'? You decide that this is a lie and that you aren't buying into it – clearly, it is you. You sentence yourself to days and weeks of endless questioning, as if you are on trial for destroying the relationship which was the very thing you loved and wanted to last forever. You get stuck because of a broken heart.

What is it about me they didn't like? What did I do wrong? Was it something I said? Was I no good?

Whether it is a relationship break-up or a best friend who suddenly starts ghosting you, you wonder where it all went wrong. You replay the last encounters you had together, forensically seeking answers.

Whenever a person rejects you, be it a friend or partner, the pain is very real, especially when you cared about and valued what you had with them. They break up with you and you don't really know all the reasons why, so you analyse every encounter you had with them in order to find a shred of reason as to why they don't want you anymore. You wind up back where you started, none the wiser. You ask your friends what they think.

Does anyone besides the person who rejected you know why it didn't work out? And if they did know, would they tell you? Chances are they wouldn't. So, after a glass or two of wine, you text your now ex-partner and try to find out the real story. You wake up the next day, remember what you did, and feel deeply embarrassed.

How do you move on?

They say that time is a healer. Recovering from heartbreak is a fight. It is a process consisting of hard work. Heartbreak has all the hallmarks of grief and loss. Later in this chapter, we will look at how to heal a broken heart.

HAVE YOU EVER FELT FORGOTTEN?

I received an email one day from a woman we'll call Caroline. The email was brief but one thing she wrote struck me. Here is an excerpt from the email:

> I have put off getting in touch with you for a long time. But something kept calling me back to write to you. To be honest I don't know if you can help or if I even deserve to be happy anymore. I feel forgotten by everyone.

Her email went on to explain how she was the victim of domestic abuse by a man she thought loved her. She had attempted to leave him a few times, but it was futile as he would manipulate her into coming back, making empty promises of change. He was narcissistic and controlling. When he was good to her he treated her like a queen, but he also could turn into a bully. Whenever she disagreed with him she became a target of gaslighting and abuse.

From a young age she had always felt like the below average girl. Her parents were very strict and would always highlight her failings and compare her to her brother. She felt like she didn't measure up. She wasn't particularly academic or sporty, didn't excel in anything and felt below par. Her brother was well-liked and successful, but she was just Caroline. In her teenage years she started to rebel and got in with the wrong crowd, looking for validation, to be seen. She got bad grades in school and when she hit her twenties she felt like she was just existing. The only thing she lived for was partying at the weekend, when she would have the opportunity to 'escape her boring reality', as she put it.

Then she met a guy at a party who made her feel wanted, made her feel beautiful, made her feel seen. When the relationship started it was amazing, but soon the cracks started to show. She rushed into getting married and things went downhill from there. Eventually it elevated to a level of him physically hurting her. A push, grabbing her, then a slap with the back of a hand. Until one bad night, he full-on punched her, knocking her to the ground.

After a visit to A&E she knew this couldn't continue but staying with him felt like the lesser of two evils. Eventually, however, she realised that he would probably kill her if she stayed.

The narcissist

Over time, Caroline had been isolated and pulled away from any support she ever had. Slowly and slyly, her husband turned her against everyone that had any positive influence over her. He was a master at creating believable stories that told her that these people, whom she had respect for, were actually trying to control her. It was easy to see he was a narcissist. Narcissists will gradually pull you away from everyone they feel has influence in your life, because they want full control. They want you to be a submissive follower. They hate people who challenge them or whom they cannot control or influence. For Caroline, he got to work slowly and subtly, turning her on those she loved.

Her family had tried to flag him to her, but in the early days she was besotted with him and thought they didn't know him like she did. She would defend him to them, standing up for him and even covering up his mistreatment. Fast forward to our sessions, and she now felt guilty, as though it was her fault everything was like this. She had lost her supportive friends and family. She felt so alone, she felt so stupid that she never saw him for what he was. She felt as if the world had forgotten about her, and that she deserved it. Caroline was stuck in a toxic relationship and didn't even know it – that is, until 15 seconds changed everything.

The 15 seconds that changed everything

After a number of years of the situation getting worse, she began to feel that he could one day kill her. The happy Caroline that had once existed had now become a fearful, nervous shell of a woman. Then one day she saw a video that a friend shared online that I had created on Instagram. The video was me sharing why every human being is valuable. It was those 15 seconds that made her reach out. Her instinct whispered 'there is hope'. She thought to herself, 'Why not send a message? What's the worst that could happen?'

Our first session was over zoom and when her camera came on I could see the remnants of the black eye that she was trying to conceal with her hair and make-up, but there was no hiding her bloodshot eye and bruising. She shared how afraid she was of him and how several times she had attempted to get help, but he would find out and explode. But by now she had had enough. It became clear she had a very low opinion of herself.

Narcissistic dynamics

When we emerge from a controlling dynamic, we can often feel stuck or lost. This is because for so long we were controlled and made to believe the other person is superior to us and we are inferior to them. There are two types of control. The first and most common is a controlling person. They are this way because they fear change or unpredictability. So, they try to control everything and everyone. They fear uncertainty because the unknown makes them feel anxious. It could be a person's behaviour or environment that they wish to control. This control is born out of fear.

The second type of control comes from a far more sinister manipulator – a narcissist. Narcissism is a self-centred personality style characterised as having an excessive preoccupation with oneself and one's own needs, often at the expense of others. It is a spectrum disorder, meaning that it can range from mild to severe. People with narcissism may have an inflated sense of importance, a deep need for admiration and a lack of empathy for others. They may also be manipulative, exploitative and vindictive.

Caroline was dealing with a narcissist. Narcissism can occur in relationships, friendships and families. I've seen it happen everywhere, from parents to spouses to bosses. When you are exposed to a behaviour or atmosphere of control and manipulation, it will gradually break you down and your confidence will diminish.

You are left feeling that you need them to survive. A narcissist doesn't want you standing on your own two feet, they need you to need them. The constant nitpicking and highlighting of your flaws and weaknesses can make you feel like a failure, or stupid.

Narcissists are so concerned about themselves that they go through life trying to control everyone else's view of them. They will treat you amazingly well to win you over as long as you have something they need. This could be your empathy or perhaps something that aids their agenda or helps their image. Narcissists are far more than just controlling, they can cause a lot of self-doubt and hurt over time.

The reality is that narcissists are generally very insecure, but to hide this they have learned to manipulate people to get what they want. They put people down and control them to puff themselves up. They love it when you need them, as it makes them feel almost like they are your god. A person can be controlling and not narcissistic, so don't jump to labelling people who might appear controlling with the name narcissist.

When someone controls you, they make you feel paralysed, like you can't do anything without their consent. It's a form of feeling stuck.

Gaslighting

Gaslighting is a term used to describe how a person manipulates you by trying to convince you that how you feel is not true or in touch with reality. Phrases such as 'you're so paranoid', 'you're mad', 'that's not how it happened', 'it wasn't like that', and 'that's not what I said' can fall under the umbrella of gaslighting. A gaslighter is trying to cause you to doubt your version of events in order to manipulate you into thinking the way that they wish you to think. They don't want you to grow or change, because that could mean you won't need them anymore and they will lose you. If you would like a deep dive into gaslighting, check out my podcast at www.markfennell.ie where I have episodes devoted to the topics of gaslighting and narcissism.

Why you can't leave

You may be in a toxic relationship with a partner, family member or friend. On one side it can give you something you crave, like feeling loved, wanted, seen or simply not alone. It gives you a way to feel something of value to you, so you put up with the pain and abuse because you feel being alone would be more painful. Or perhaps telling the world that your marriage failed, or that you are estranged from your family member, would be more painful than the abuse itself.

On the other side, what we don't realise is that we are being slowly broken down and toxic behaviour is conditioning us to believe we need that person. The very person who is dealing out the hurt is the one we feel we need. It's complete manipulation. If you ever feel you need a person who is mistreating you, it warrants asking yourself, 'Am I truly happy? Why do I tolerate this?'

It is like Stockholm syndrome, a term used to describe how hostage takers will win over the hostages to their frame of mind, even convincing the hostages to sympathise with and help their captors.

A person stays in a relationship because they feel it is the best of a bad situation and that the alternative of leaving would be worse. The truth is, the pain of leaving a toxic relationship will subside, but the pain from the abuse will get worse in time and will be like having a weight around your life. If you are a victim of a toxic relationship, please get help.

Caroline was stuck because she felt low self-esteem prior to meeting her husband, he exploited this and created an environment in which she needed him in order to feel loved. The work I did with Caroline was around identity and seeing that it started with her realising that self-worth doesn't come from other people's opinions, but from within. We must learn to love ourselves and not rely on the love of others to define our self-worth. We looked at every stage of identity and worked on addressing the ones that needed altering.

Caroline made the **decision** to stay even though she felt so broken, because she couldn't imagine being okay alone. She felt that she would be forgotten. That potential pain of loneliness was greater than the pain of the abuse. Here **decisions**, **actions** and the **habit** of staying were because her view of herself, her **identity**. She said that she was nothing without this man. That is what we got to work on with Caroline.

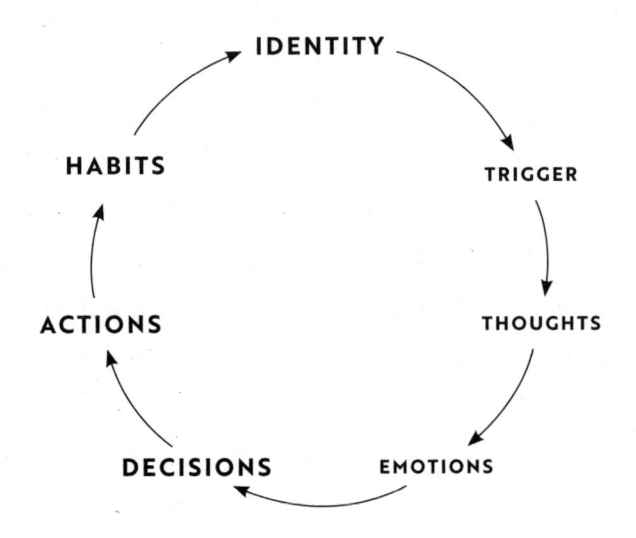

IDENTITY → TRIGGER → THOUGHTS → EMOTIONS → DECISIONS → ACTIONS → HABITS → IDENTITY

We started by pretending there was a blank canvas and I asked her that if she had the power to create any life and identity for herself what would it look like. She described a happy healthy woman living a life that had purpose and people who loved her. This was an identity that she would love.

We then used the WCPT method followed by the XYZ method (both outlined in chapter 1) to start ironing out the issues and limiting beliefs. False beliefs like 'I'm not enough' became a belief of 'I am no less than anyone else and that's a fact'. Simultaneously she created a reason why she deserved to have a life she loved. Within six months she was a new person.

She went to college, started on a successful career and has recently met someone who, as she says, 'knows how to love me for me'. Love builds you up as a person, it doesn't tear you down.

A broken heart can love again

It was hard for Caroline to love again because that meant trusting and being vulnerable. But a broken heart can love again. The idea of going through all the motions of getting to know each other, the dates, the chats, the hard work to try and see if it's worth a go, can leave a person stuck. If you've been hurt, why would you go through all that work and effort again when there is a risk that it could hurt you and end in failure? So you get stuck into your job or career, distracting yourself from the idea that you want a relationship but just aren't bothered to keep trying. You try a few dating apps, swipe on potentials, and head off on dates, only to realise that a lot of people just want the sex and not the relationship you long for. You delete the app and go back to your career.

Then after time passes, you start to see friends coupling up, and you don't want to be left single – so off you go again.

Dealing with the pain of a broken heart is one element, but having the motivation to put the work into a future relationship is the other. Whatever has happened to you, the first thing to getting unstuck is taking a step.

Many people feel stuck, but some also feel they don't deserve any better. A baby step is better than no step at all. Even if you feel you are crawling in the right direction, any movement can be the beginning of your new path. Even the fact you are reading this book tells me there is something within you trying to find a solution to an area of your life, and I commend you for that. But always remember, your future happiness is not reliant on others, it is reliant on what you do next.

THE NINE KEYS TO HEALING YOUR HEART

Healing a broken heart has no definitive timescale. It takes as long as it takes, but the key is to not dwell in misery. There is a time to process, but try to prevent that time becoming so long that years begin to stack up. I say this because a broken heart can define us if we allow it. We can take on the mentality that we are rejected goods for whatever reason, and live our lives in that mindset. Rejection by someone does not make you a reject, it just means you weren't for them. The reason a heartbreak hurts so much is because the rejection is coming from someone we love. But it is also the disappointment that the dream and plans that we had with that person are all gone into oblivion. It hurts to be hurt. I have here nine keys to help you heal from a broken heart when you feel the time is right and you are ready.

1. Let them go

Make the decision that it is time to let them go. If you are still connected to them due to co-parenting, or you see them at work, or they live near you, it is still time to let them go. We are the ones that hold onto them mentally and emotionally, and it doesn't just stop. It is not easy considering this person was your partner, lover and friend who knew everything about you. But you need to decide to remove them from this position in your life. They may have a part of your life still, but they are not defining of your future life. Let them go because that is best for you and them. As long as you are holding them in an important place in your life, they may influence it and prevent you from moving on.

2. Remove the visuals

Remove any photos of you together that might be hanging in your room or house. These can act like subconscious triggers. If there are kids involved, you can possibly put the photos in their rooms, but take them out of prominent positions of eye contact for you and visitors to the house. These images don't help you move on. They stay as a potential reminder of pain and old memories can subconsciously keep you repeating the story that this happiness is gone. Images of you together online should be hidden so that you don't see them without choosing to. I once had a client who felt he was over his break up but kept feeling sad when he sat in his living room. It turned out there was a photo of his ex on the wall that he had forgotten about. When he removed the photo, the negative feelings in that room went away over time. Don't underestimate your subconscious.

3. Time to unfriend

The social media connections have to be cut. It might be hard to see what the harm is if you are friends online, but the problem is that you are now in each other's business. When he or she adds a new friend, shares a photo or video, next thing you know you've spent hours wondering who that person in the photo is. You need to cut ties, otherwise you will get caught on the occasional stalking mission. Trust me, I know it sounds hard, it is hard, you will move on faster when you see their face less. If you have kids together and must be online friends for practical reasons, then mute their posts. But make sure they don't have a way to watch your life online. They are your child's parent and not your partner.

4. Boundaries

If you cross paths with them often or have friends in common, you may not want boundaries. But in order to heal, you have to put them in place. Boundaries have proven to be the universal tip for co-parenting couples or former couples who still come into contact, for whatever reason. Boundaries include decisions to exert self-control when you see them – for example, keeping things civil but not engaging in full-on conversations about how they are and what they've been up to.

If you work together, don't be having lunch together, and if conversations arise keep them short but not inquisitive. I know you want to know what they are up to but trust me, this is only torturing yourself. If you are in a co-parenting situation, there has to be an agreement to talk only about the kids and if texts or calls are made, they are purely about the children. If boundaries aren't in place, problems arise when one of the parents wants to ask questions about the other's personal life, like 'Who was that parked outside the other day?' or 'Are you seeing someone?' It's easiest to put boundaries in place from the start in order to prevent such awkward conversations. It also stops you asking about their lives, which would in fact prevent you from moving on. Sometimes moving job or house is necessary if you cross paths a lot. A change in location can help you heal and move on.

5. The blame game

Self-blame is sometimes a real struggle for some. We pick our personal poison, which we consume by the bucket. We default to 'it's me, not them'. If you have been rejected or abused in your younger years, you can now feel that this is the same old story repeating itself, rejected again. You may wonder what is wrong with you. You weren't the one for them and that is sometimes how cruel life can be. But it doesn't mean that you are damaged goods. They didn't see the amazing human being you are, and that's okay. It doesn't change anything about your future, except the fact they are the one you won't be spending it with. Remind yourself that no relationship is perfect, so stop remembering it like it was. You are painting an untrue picture of what you had, giving it a meaning that might not be accurate.

6. Distract when triggered

When you are triggered, you need to have a 'go-to' plan ready and loaded. PDF from the last chapter is ideal. Have an intentional thing you will do in the event of being triggered so you are prepared. For example, a woman I coached would always think of her ex at lunchtime, because they always had lunch together as their offices were beside each other. This was actually how they met. So when it was close to one o'clock she would always be triggered with a thought of him. We created a 'go to' by setting an alarm for 12:55 p.m. so that she could call a colleague or friend for a chat. Or she would invite one of her colleagues for lunch. This new habit broke the cycle and after a long period of time it became her new habit. She didn't even realise she had forgotten about her ex at lunch till I asked her months later.

7. Draw friends close

Social support has proven to be vital in recovering from heartbreak. Having someone we can simply vent to is crucial. It may be a friend, family member, life coach or therapist. But having someone you can confide in is so important and proven to help you heal. Talking is therapy.

8. Routine

Keeping a simple routine is paramount. Go easy on yourself and don't overwhelm yourself with distractions. But keep getting up and going about your day even when you don't feel like it. Cultivate a routine that helps you to take the space and time out for yourself when you just need to have a good cry. This doesn't mean allowing yourself to stay in bed all day – when we stay in bed our pain gets worse as heartbreak becomes all we can think about; is consumes us. Keep a simple routine of getting up and getting out. Go walking, to the gym, or for coffee with friends. Try to avoid the temptation to just stop everything.

9. Forgiveness

This is sometimes needed in two directions: forgiving yourself and forgiving them. Sometimes this is thought of as letting the person off the hook. There is some truth to that, but the greater truth about forgiveness is that it doesn't mean that the other person has been let away with what they did; it just means that you aren't holding onto what they did to you anymore. This allows you to move on. You need to forgive yourself for the times you put yourself down, blamed yourself and you told yourself you are no good. Forgive yourself for treating yourself like that. Forgive yourself for being in a failed relationship and for any feelings of letting your family or kids down. Forgiveness is very tough to do, especially when you are on the receiving end of the pain and feel you did nothing wrong. But there also comes a time when we blame ourselves, and to move on from that we must forgive ourselves. I'll elaborate on forgiveness in chapter 13 and explain why forgiveness is massive in healing.

WHY DO YOU WANT TO LOVE AGAIN?

Like all forms of stuck, we must ask ourselves what is on the other side of being relationally stuck. When it comes to a new relationship, start visualising the life you want. Pretend if you must that you are a blank canvas, with no baggage, past pain or heartbreak. With that mindset, figure out what you want and why. This is what you get to work on visualising for yourself. Acknowledge that you may have come through a storm and you don't feel like loving again, but that the long-term view of your life tells a different story. It says that although you feel stuck and hurt now, how would you feel in five or even ten years' time if you did nothing? It is with that state of mind you get to work – for the sake of your future self.

Olivia was very hurt and angry. She was bitter with everyone due to the pain she went through. When we got to work, she realised that she had become someone she didn't recognise and didn't want to be any longer. In time she made a shift in her attitude towards love and other people. Funnily enough, after joining a charity walk, she got talking with a guy. Three years later they were married with a baby on the way. A charity walk became a massive step in her life all because she changed from being a victim of circumstance to a victor mindset.

It will be hard to move forward, but it will be worth it. You deserve to be loved and you have love to give. Love is a gift to be treasured and if you want it, then you have the power to receive it. When we start to walk in love, it is amazing how we then attract it. That is exactly what happened my client.

Walking in love will make you more attractive than hurt or bitterness ever could. You decide who you become.

You are a priceless masterpiece because the world gets only one of you.

Being relationally stuck can occur for different reasons. Maybe you feel you are attracting the wrong people or you avoid dating altogether in order to avoid being rejected. Or maybe you've given up and feel stuck because you feel everyone decent is already taken. These narratives can govern us, but maybe you feel that now is the time to change them. Change is possible. When you feel ready to put yourself out there into the wild west called the dating game, you may lack motivation, which is completely understandable. Sometimes a real roadblock I see is when clients have a perfect picture in their mind of what their life should be and with whom. Sometimes they haven't met the person yet, but they have this list of boxes to be ticked. As time goes by, this list has caused them to block out practically everyone they have met. My advice is to always have an open mind when it comes to finding that special someone. Rather than focusing on your entire list, focus on your values. This is far more fruitful. Values, as we have discussed, are the things we hold very dear to us.

Relationship values

Values are the bedrock upon which we build our lives. Values such as integrity, respect and gratitude serve as our moral compass, guiding us through the challenges we face and illuminating the path we trust as our truth. These are the ideals that shape our lives and define us. There are also relationship values that are essential and can serve as a strong foundation, guiding us towards true love.

MUTUAL RESPECT is a fundamental pillar upon which healthy relationships thrive. It is the recognition and admiration of each other's worth, opinions, boundaries and differences.

HONESTY is a bedrock value. Open and truthful communication encourages vulnerability, and a deep connection between two people.

TRUST builds bridges, allowing us to rely on one another, knowing that we have each other's backs through thick and thin.

COMPASSION is a value that should resonate within a relationship. It involves showing kindness, empathy, and understanding towards our partner's feelings.

EQUALITY is a non-negotiable value in a healthy partnership. It is the recognition and respect for each other's autonomy, opinions, and rights, ensuring a balance.

SHARED VISION AND GOALS form the ties that bind two hearts together. When we align our visions and aspirations, we embark on a journey of growth, support, and shared accomplishments.

INTIMACY goes beyond physical connection. Emotional intimacy is the ability to be vulnerable, to truly know and be known by our partner. It is a precious gift that fosters deeper understanding and love.

COMPROMISE is the art of finding common ground, seeking solutions that honour the needs and desires of both individuals, fostering harmony and understanding.

FRIENDSHIP is a treasure that enhances any romantic relationship. It is the genuine liking, camaraderie, and companionship that we share with our partner, forming a solid basis for lasting love.

LAUGHTER is a value that is often overlooked. A shared sense of humour and the ability to find joy in each other's company can truly brighten a relationship.

These values are the building blocks of a strong and fulfilling relationship. As you seek love, remember to focus on your values for they will guide you towards a partnership that nourishes and uplifts both of you. You will lean more towards some than others.

You can also use the values exercise in chapter 2, and have it in mind when creating a dating app profile or talking to potential partners. Find out what they value and see if you are in alignment.

One tip I share with anyone going dating is to see it as an opportunity to make a friend and have a laugh. Sometimes people can go straight into serious questions like 'How many kids do you want?', and generally this is too much too fast.

Give yourself a chance

Everyone deserves a second chance at love (and maybe even a third, fourth and so on). Even though you might feel that a specific person was the one, I can certainly say with hand on heart there will always be another 'one' if you let yourself be open. It is our own selves that hold us back.

> **There is more than one version of 'happily ever after' for each of us.**

Life is rarely straightforward, so don't let all your hopes and dreams go just because a relationship didn't work out. You have a choice. Ask yourself: 'Do I want to love again, or do I want to stay stuck in love with the idea that that person was the only one?' If you want to love again then set it as your desire and you will find someone who wants to love you right back. Seek and ye will find.

THE GREATEST RESEARCH ON RELATIONSHIPS

What is the key to a healthy relationship that will last the test of time? This is the million-dollar question asked by couples or those seeking to find a partner. The other thing people often ask is how to stop their relationship from getting stale or boring. In this section we will look at the answers to both those questions.

It's the little things

The Gottman Institute is for me the gold standard in relationship wisdom. They ran a study of thousands of couples to find out if there is a way to indicate if a couple will divorce. Among their findings was the fact that the level of connection a couple has is a precursor to the health of that relationship. The small things, whether positive or negative, are the tell-tale signs.

For example, a partner comes home and says they are tired from work. The partner at home looking after the kids all day responds, 'I'm tired too,' and doesn't ask what has happened to their partner that has made them tired. The partner coming home doesn't feel listened to, and therefore this has a negative impact on their connection. Connection is when we feel a person cares for us, has an interest in us, and we feel listened to. These micro displays of connection over time are markers for the health of a couple's relationship. The small signals that show we care and are interested in our partner are essential to long-term relationship health. When a relationship becomes stuck or has lost its spark, getting back to those acts of interest and kindness can help with reuniting. Perhaps you are both tired, but you are also a team, so look after each other, listen to each other, and take care of each other.

The key to great sex

Relationships can be bumpy and a perfect one doesn't exist. They can sometimes even go a little stale. I have seen people get through the bumpiest of trials and tribulations because they shared some core values, like laughter, honesty and mutual respect. Relationships are ultimately intimate deep friendships. When a person feels unfulfilled in their relationship, or when it has lost its spark, there is a sense of being stuck in a rut. How do you get out of such a rut?

Maybe you have busy careers, or babies to look after that leave you both exhausted after a day's work. You barely have time to talk, let alone have sex, so instead you pop on the TV to wind down and then go to bed to sleep. When the spark feels extinguished, you need to work on what brings you together; it is that togetherness that forms connection. People don't fall out of love, they disconnect and love leaves. According to the Gottman Institute, the best thing a couple can do to have a great sex life and keep the spark alive is to invest in the quality of their friendship. It's a simple, almost basic tip that I can testify has saved many a relationship and marriage. Naturally, other factors matter, but the most important one clearly identified is the quality of their friendship, or in other words, connection. Sex after all is the physical manifestation of deep connection. Plan a date night, go to a comedy club, hike or have a picnic. Share experiences that you can talk about and that rekindle connection. Make space for each other, have deep as well as light-hearted conversations. Get back to those micro displays of affection and consideration. Don't give up because it feels stuck, instead rekindle. When you are best friends, it keeps connection alive.

STUCK BECAUSE OF SOCIETY

Every day we are bombarded with what's in, what's on trend and what society expects of us at certain points in our lives – it's this in your twenties, that in your thirties or this in your forties, etc.

This pressure to conform to what some call 'normal' can bring with it pressure, guilt and even feelings of failure. You can feel stuck because you don't want to be in the stream of life that is deemed 'what you should do or be'. In fact, you want to travel, you don't want to get married and kids are still a maybe in your mind. Parents and peers all have an opinion of who and what you should be. This is a kind of relationally stuck because you don't want to be in a stereotypical romantic relationship and yet feel judged by society.

Catherine felt really guilty because her business was her baby, and she didn't want to get married or have kids. She felt like if she did it would be for her mother's sake and not hers. When her sister had a baby, she realised parenting wasn't for her and she decided to never make the mistake of trying to fit a mould that her heart wasn't in.

THE ONE PATH MYTH

There is a term used in psychology called the one path myth. This is essentially the belief a person holds that there is only one way to be happy, and they subsequently believe that happiness is exclusively linked to a certain person, house, job, and so on. A person can get stuck with an idealised belief that there is only one road to happiness with one particular person. This person is 'the one' and there is no other like them. Then if the relationship fails, they cannot envision ever being happy again. I think that we should be slow to call someone the one, because it leads us to believe that there is *only* that person for us. Ultimately, there are many paths that can take us to the same destination; we might just need to reroute.

Believing that a certain person was the 'only one' is actually a limiting belief. Then when it fails to work out, that belief tells us that all other options are secondary, and so now that the number one choice is gone, we have no chance of ever being happy. People become relationally stuck because they feel there was only one way to be happy and so they struggle to love again.

It is to do with the finite view that it was them or nothing. You had this relationship that made you so happy, and now that it is gone, so too is your level of happiness. Trying to connect with new people on dates proves hard because it is clearly not at the level of depth as to the relationship you came from. So you give up, thinking that you don't connect with anyone else like you did with your ex. The truth is that depth happens over time, so you have to go through the stages of a relationship to forge that trust and vulnerability. Maybe the love you experienced in that previous relationship was the most you ever felt, but you might experience even more with the right person in your future. Even though that relationship was good, your next relationship might be even better. So, when you have to sit through those dates that won't go anywhere, don't lose heart because the next one might be the best yet.

CHAPTER 12

Interpersonally stuck: friends and frenemies

I'LL BE THERE FOR YOU ... LIKE YOU'RE THERE FOR ME TOO

Friends. Why is a show about a group of people living close to each other and drinking coffee a lot of the time so popular? The jokes, the funny stories, the love story of Rachel and Ross? It is because the show is relatable and captures what we all want: a group of friends who accept us as we are and are always there for us. Regardless of what they got up to, they always had love and respect towards each other.

I mention this because it is so important to be mindful of the company we keep. The people we hold near to us impact our thoughts and feelings; they influence how we see things. Surrounding ourselves with positive influences is vital. People can help us maintain a healthy mindset and emotional well-being, or they can do the opposite.

The right people will share your rhythm. There won't need to be a discussion on how things should be in the friendship, it will just flow, just click. Not everyone you are friends with will click on this level, and that's okay and normal too. Your close friends will probably be countable on one hand by a certain age. They will be the people who really get you. The older you get, the more friendships are about quality over quantity.

> **Haters talk about where you've been, critics talk about where you're going, good friends are there, wherever you're at.**

Personality type plays a role when it comes to connecting, but the reason we will click with certain people on a slightly deeper level is because of beliefs and values: the inner convictions that are almost like our own rules for life. This includes what we believe about important topics and whatever is important to us. When we find friends who share our values, it can elicit a strong connection.

BELIEFS AND VALUES

Our beliefs and values shape us from a young age. We are influenced by parents, teachers and peers, whose words hold great power. For instance, when a frustrated teacher tells us we'll never succeed, it can leave a lasting impact. Even in adulthood, that belief echoes, influencing our actions. Beliefs become deeply rooted in our minds and are often mistaken for facts.

What failing taught me

I didn't like history; in fact I would often fall asleep during the class. In the run up to the Junior Certificate, I failed the mock exam. The teacher pulled me aside and said: 'You are not good at history, but if you were just a bit better at it you could get a C.' I realised he had faith in me, and it had a profound impact. I knew that reading the history book would consistently lull me to sleep so in a stroke of innovation, I devised a solution. I began recording myself reading the important sections aloud, and I would listen to them while going to school or lying in bed before sleep. This routine continued for months, as I aimed for a modest C grade on the upcoming exam. My teacher's belief in my abilities had made a significant difference. He encouraged me, emphasising that I only needed to improve slightly. His belief in me became my own. I wholeheartedly embraced the belief that all I needed was to be a little better.

The exam came around and I showed up feeling 50/50 about the whole thing, but I repeated a mantra that my mum had always said to me:

It's not about being the best, it's about simply doing your best.

I completed the exam, and I didn't get a C, or even a B. In fact, I got an A. I actually aced the exam. I couldn't believe it. My mum and teacher couldn't believe it either.

What I didn't realise then was that the teacher's belief in me was enough of a spark to push me to try harder. But he also made it achievable by telling me to go for the C, as the A was a mile off. What if he had not bothered to pull me aside, or worse again had told me I'd never be good at history? I could have had a very different relationship with the subject. I share this story with people who manage, lead, or educate. When people allow you influence over their lives, you are in a privileged position and should not misuse this influence.

It was not just this lesson I learned from not quitting. It also showed me not to settle for mediocrity in any area of life. Because I spent months listening back to myself, I started to hear how I spoke and noticed things I didn't like. This helped me to improve how I spoke. I believe wholeheartedly that little pushes of support like the one from the teacher brought me to a place where I was confident with public speaking. I learned so many lessons that had nothing to do with history because of one teacher encouraging me to do a little better. I developed a way to listen to myself reading and the domino effect led to me being on radio years later, having my own podcast, and writing this book. Without that teacher I would have never hit record on that tape deck, and who knows how different life could have been. When I was recording, I never fell asleep while reading, so nowadays when I really want to learn something I will read it out loud (much to the annoyance of Fiona) and it sticks.

Parents and teachers are hugely influential, but so are our friends. We sometimes need only one cheerleader to encourage us through a tough time, it doesn't have be a squad of people. But the opposite is also true: it can take only one person or even one bad comment to send us on a spiral downward. I've coached many public figures over the years and I have seen that all the praise they receive is great, but it can be overshadowed by one nasty comment or article, even when the vast majority of people support them. Part of my job is helping people to get to a place of not caring about the negative stuff and staying the course.

Show me your friends and I'll show you your future

They say we become the sum of the five people closest to us. It is the people in our lives that have a direct influence in shaping us as people. I'm not suggesting you start cutting people out of your life, but maybe it is worth looking at limiting your time spent with them. Work towards lowering the volume on negative people and introducing people who will bring insight, encouragement and wisdom into your life. Be aware of who you invest your time with. Sometimes you have to make your circles smaller so that your vision can get bigger.

Family are the people we love and they are also some of the most influential people in our lives. So if sibling rivalry exists it won't be helpful when you have good news to share and they get jealous. Keep things functional and take note of the off-limit areas or topics. Sometimes a person will do anything to make their parents happy and it can lead to inner pain when the love is not reciprocated or they are even rejected.

Consider the following questions:
- Are you trying to make someone like you but they don't?
- Do you want them to love you back but they never show it?
- Do you want support but never get it?

We can't make anyone, let alone family, do any of the above, so you must protect yourself and your peace and remember it is their issue. Don't make it yours and love them from afar if necessary.

Mindsets can be inherited. A bitter parent can spread their views to their children and they too can become bitter. You must guard yourself against negative influences for the sake of your future happiness. Your vibe attracts your tribe. If your instinct is calling you towards good things and the people around you are saying it's too risky, then you might never take the leap. But if you spend time around those that spur you on, just think what you could achieve.

One major reason people get stuck is due to the company they keep. A person who is bitter or envious with the world generally won't like people who are doing well or loving life. This is why haters exist online and behind closed doors. It is because they are envious of people who have what they feel they should have. People hurt others because they are hurting. If you have someone like this as a friend, they will no doubt limit you. This sounds harsh but sadly it is true, and we sometimes have to be honest with ourselves and look at who we spend time with. Do they help or hinder your confidence and joy?

The backstabber

Tom had a dear friend named Peter. He took him under his wing and trained him in his area of business. Then one day, things changed. The conversations were shorter, the random funny texts stopped. Tom felt that their friendship was a one-way street, with him always going to Peter and no reciprocation. What Tom didn't know was that Peter had gone behind his back and undercut him by taking a large contract Tom had been negotiating. What Peter didn't know is that Tom would have gone in with him on the contract if he had come and spoken to him about it. He felt like he had been stabbed in the back. Overnight, after years of friendship, he was gone.

On reflection, Tom realised he had missed his falseness and soon could see that Peter had had an agenda from the start. He had used Tom as his stepping stone in his career. All Tom did was help the guy, and then when he had no more need of him, he was gone. But it taught Tom so much. Sometimes the closest people to us hurt us the most. I love this quote because it says so much:

When people don't support you publicly, maybe it's because of what they said about you privately.

Tom was now faced with a choice. Should he become bitter and stop mentoring people for fear he raise up another backstabber? Should he tell the world what Peter did to him? A part of him wanted to go to Peter and speak his mind, but his heart said let it go. Peter knew what he did was bad form. Tom forgave him and let it go, as hard as that was.

Sticks and stones may break my bones but words can kill

Adam became the target of vicious online bullying, filled with hurtful and insulting remarks towards him and his family. The level of cruelty displayed went beyond mere jealousy; it was genuine hatred.

In a moment of vulnerability, he made the mistake of reading comments someone had sent him, only to discover that they were deeply personal and malicious. It was clear that someone close to him was involved, which made the situation even more devastating. The experience plunged him into a state of despair and shook his confidence. He had a very public position and so this was in his face every day.

Adam became very stuck. At one point, he found it so hard that thoughts of ending his life became a very real option. He feared he would never escape the onslaught of online abuse and it followed him around. Thankfully, through weekly sessions with me, he got his spark back eventually and got out of that dark time. Today he is doing incredibly well and the situation didn't go in the sad direction that some others have due to online hate.

The reason I share Adam's story is because we all know what it's like to be on the receiving end of hurtful comments. I'm sure you've heard the countless stories of online abuse in schools and the workplace. But the lesson is, when people throw hurtful comments to your face or behind your back, it's rarely about you. It has more to do with their unhappiness. When a person truly cares for you, they might say things that hurt, but they will move to rectify it in some way in time. Similarly, if you did wrong and hurt someone you truly care about, you'll make an effort to restore things. So if you feel stuck because of hurt from a friend, a partner or a colleague and they never made any moves to restore things, maybe it's time to realise that they don't care enough for your relationship. In fact, if they don't see your value then they are not right for you. I know it hurts, but that pain will keep you stuck unless you let it go.

Generally, when people operate in the shadows it is because their behaviour would be viewed as sinister if done in public and they know it. Even more reason to be wary of being close with such people. When we are victims of hurt, we can get stuck there. But as I said to one particular client who had colleagues use her as a scapegoat and for no reason other than to save themselves from their mistakes: You have a choice. Do you value getting revenge even more than you value your peace and integrity? Do you want revenge to take your focus, or do you want to heal? Does hurting them back make you a happy person? The ultimate revenge is soaring above what they have done and becoming your best successful self.

Our values are key in decision making. Look back at the values you identified for yourself in chapter 2. You decide what you value most, and it will decide your next move. You can get bitter or you can get better.

The ego wants revenge because it is appalled by how they dared to treat you. How dare they spread rumours about you? But it is incredibly freeing not to care. I understand that if it's a legal scenario or defamation then it's different. But even at that level you can take the relevant action but still have a view that literally doesn't care. There is liberty in that.

A STUDY ON REVENGE

A group of Swiss researchers scanned the brains of people who had been wronged during an economic exchange game.[6] These people had trusted their partners to split a pot of money with them, only to find that the partners had chosen to keep the loot for themselves. The researchers then gave the people a chance to punish their greedy partners, and for a full minute, as the victims contemplated revenge, the activity in their brains was recorded. The decision caused a rush of neural activity in the caudate nucleus, an area of the brain known to process rewards. The findings, published in a 2004 issue of *Science*, gave physiological confirmation to what the scorned have been saying for years: revenge is sweet. The study showed that while participants felt this initial happiness at the prospects of revenge, when the actual revenge was acted upon it did little in resolving the offence. In other words, the idea of taking revenge gives us pleasure as opposed to the act, which is quite the contrary. I liken it to the person on a diet who is tempted by food they know they shouldn't eat. They really want it and salivate at the idea of how tasty it will be. But after they consume it, they feel even worse than before.

A higher valued response

Revenge may provide temporary satisfaction, but it does not

remedy the hurt or help you heal. Revenge often leads to a cycle of retaliation. Revenge leads to unhappiness. Revenge keeps what the offender has done on repeat only causing you to get stuck there. Being stuck in the emotional state of feeling you were a victim leads to frustration, anger and sadness, which can culminate in bitterness. The simple truth is that revenge won't make anything better, it will in fact prolong the hurt and turn it into anger. Try and rise above it. Rising above the temptation to seek revenge happens when we value our peace more than their words; when we value integrity more than being cruel; when we value our well-being more than trying to affect theirs. Be the better person and in the long term, you'll come out on top.

People dislike others for many reasons but three common ones are:

1. They are envious or jealous of you. They want what you have.
2. They don't like you, maybe because of how you look, where you're from or your personality.
3. Lack of achievement. When they see your achievements, they see what they could have had. Seeing you reminds them of their own lack of achievement in life.

THE GOOD NEWS

Let's look at how to get unstuck from hurt and pain with a view to keeping us from getting stuck in the future. Friends (and I mean good friends) are hard to find. But friends can be the ultimate accountability partners and can even help us to get unstuck. Sometimes it's better to have a friend nearby than a brother far away. Friends can be like family. There are some things to remember that I would consider a help when it comes to friends.

Trust some people, but not everybody

Trust is built over time and can be destroyed in a moment. But it is important to let people in so you can build up trust. It can be hard to trust again when your trust was broken by someone close to you, but give people a chance and you might find a new friend. Something I have had to learn is that I trust people too quickly. Trust gets built over time and you shouldn't give too much away too soon. But sometimes we get stuck not trusting anyone because of past hurt. Learning to trust again is important, so take it slowly. Trust has levels to it.

Know people by what they do more than by what they say

Friends prove themselves by their actions as opposed to their words. Look for the people who show they care, not just say they care. A random 'how are you' text, the buying of an unsuspected gift, treating you to a meal or even a real hug can say a lot. This can help you see who your close friends are but also see who may not be there for you. Don't get stuck thinking they are your bestie when maybe they are a frenemy. Actions are telling. The same is true for you. Maybe a friend hasn't shown they cared, but that doesn't mean you shouldn't show them. When you start acting in a caring way, it might trigger their reciprocation. Treat people like you would like to be treated. This can help in building friendships. Dale Carnegie, an American writer and lecturer who was best known for his book *How to Win Friends and Influence People*, said:

> **You can make more friends in two months by becoming interested in other people than you can in two years by trying to get other people interested in you.**

Don't expect you from them. People have their own way of doing things

Friends won't always react like you would and that's okay. Don't set your standards on them, for we are all different. People react to things differently and that doesn't mean you can't be friends. In fact, it can be eye-opening. Learning how others think could open your thinking to different mindsets to learn from. We can sometimes get stuck thinking one way, but friends introduce to us other perspectives on things.

> **You'll never heal your heart by reliving what broke it.**

If you are stuck hurting because of a friendship that failed, it's time to move on. Maybe you have tried to reach out only to be rejected once more. If you were in the wrong, say sorry and move on. It is not easy, but I have seen people get stuck reliving what hurt them for years only to find they never moved on. We'll discuss this more in the next chapter.

The more chances you give, the less respect you'll get

Chances are needed but endless chances aren't. There comes a time when you have to be real and stop allowing bad friends to hurt you over and over. You can get stuck in a pattern with people. I recall a client we'll call Henry. Henry's best friend was hooked on smoking weed. They shared an apartment which they bought together and, no matter what, he just wouldn't quit. The real problem was that Henry had asthma. He tried many times to ask his friend not to smoke in the apartment but he feared falling out with him because they split the mortgage. Fear of confrontation and the fear of being left with a hefty mortgage let the friendship go into a pattern. Henry was never listened to and over the two years of living together he had multiple asthma attacks and hated the arrangement. He was stuck.

It started to get him really down and he decided to get a life coach. We worked on a few things including self-esteem and confidence. Henry could see that fear made him tolerate behaviour that was not just bad for his health but also left him feeling belittled. It led to him staying in his room the whole time. Henry adopted a new approach that made his friend realise that he wasn't playing anymore. In a tactful, respectful way he said, 'Either you quit this in the apartment or I'll be calling the guards every time you light up.' His friend got the message and it actually resolved itself. They still share the apartment but a new-found respect is in place.

The point is, don't allow people to walk all over you when they are going against your values. If you do, you can lose the respect of those involved and those watching.

Boundaries

Perhaps you are stuck in a pattern of being hurt. You can't stop someone breaking your heart once. But you can stop them doing it again. The simple reason is, if you let them back in, then you have inadvertently given them permission to break your heart again by reinstating them in your life. If you've been hurt over and over, take a step back and identify what boundaries might be needed.

I had a client named Paul who was very empathetic. He fell in love with a girl, and she told him stories of how she needed money for her child and house. When he was slow to give money, she distanced herself from him. He then felt bad for not helping and reverted to giving her support, even though the actual father of her child was absent. She exploited his empathy and compassion. He came for coaching and raised this as a concern. It turned out there was a history of people taking his money. He had a low opinion of himself but when he helped people it gave him purpose. He was stuck in this pattern. We established boundaries and soon enough he got to see which relationships in his life were real and true. These boundaries broke the pattern. Sometimes we need boundaries to protect ourselves from the pattern of hurt.

Intention

> **Your time is limited, don't waste it living someone else's life.**
> **STEVE JOBS**

One last thing on friendship: if you feel stuck and the people in your life are partly the cause, you must be clear in your identity. Some people would rather you accommodate their identity as opposed to yours. Some people will have you live your life helping them get to where they are going and with no regard for your plans. Some will try and make you into the person they want you to be as opposed to you setting the course for your identity. Maybe it's a friend, a business partner, colleague or manager. Yes we respect all we come in contact with and in a job abide by the rules. But be clear on your intentions. Is this person bringing me in the direction I want to go. Or am I in this friendship only to accommodate their identity.

> **If you don't have a plan, you will end out helping someone with theirs.**

Be clear on your identity and be crystal clear who are the friends in your life that support your intentions. Remember our friends can help us or hinder us with our life goals, ambitions and dreams. Be careful who you allow to ride in the seat next to you on this journey called life. I'm not suggesting every friendship and person in your life is like Mr Motivator. Some people are great for a laugh, others for insight, others for support and some for a good old chat. The point I am making is find the people who like you for you and not what they can get from you.

Friends will influence the roads you take and the decisions you make.

EXERCISE
INVEST IN FRIENDSHIP

This is a very simple but effective exercise. Grab your calendar (in chapter 6 we discussed how to avoid to-do lists and plan a day and a time to do different tasks with intention). Write down one to three people who you consider true friends, based on what we learned about in this chapter. It could be someone who you know is always there for you, but maybe you don't see or speak to them much. Or someone you support but who also supports you. Now reach out to them and plan a chat, ideally face to face.

The best kind of friend is the one who comes in when the whole world has gone out.
UNKNOWN

Sometimes we need to stop in our tracks and invest our time into friendships that matter, because that is what will matter in the long term. The point of the exercise is that you are planning to surround yourself with the right people and the right influence. Intentionally choose who you invest time with so that their positive influence is the one you are feeling when you get stuck. Rather than wait until you are stuck, build that friendship now. If you are already feeling stuck, all the more reason to reach out.

What if you met this person who encourages you once a week? Just think of the positive impact it would have, especially when you need advice or encouragement. Investing time with people we respect and admire exposes us to their mindset. If you want to think like happy people, spend time with happy people. If you want focus, let focused people show you how. If you want to be successful, learn from successful people.

If you don't have someone to reach out to that you feel will be there for you, or if you are at a place in life that not many understand (like running a business), you are welcome to reach out to me and consider joining my monthly group called Tribe. Make sure you have the right people around you, who don't just tolerate you but celebrate you; people who will push and propel you to reach your full potential in life. Who you are is influenced by who you spend time with.

People may listen, but a true friend will hear you.

CHAPTER 13
Historically stuck: dealing with the past

DEALING WITH THE PAST

We all have a past, and our view of the past is the reason for how we are in our present. Historically stuck is when we find it hard to progress or grow because we find ourselves mentally spending our time revisiting our past, like a historian studying history. The past can break a person, or it can be the making of them. There is a lot to learn from the past, but our nature tends to want to focus on the negative elements of our history. We can sometimes view the past with a magnifying glass and zero in on the difficult times we experienced or the pain we endured. If you want to be better in an area of life, it may be constructive to identify whether the past has played a part in this area you feel stuck in. The past is gone, but we essentially make our past our present every time we replay it. From a troubled upbringing to bullying, failure and trauma, so many things can happen in a lifetime that can influence the trajectory of a person's well-being. In this chapter, we are going to deal with the past so that it doesn't hold you back anymore.

The only limit to your future success is the replaying of yesterday's pain.

LEARNING COMMUNICATION AND BUILDING RESPECT: HARRY'S STORY

Harry was a married man struggling with anger issues and a deep desire for respect. He reached out to me for assistance in improving his communication and restoring harmony within his family. His frustration stemmed from feeling unheard and disrespected by his wife, Caitríona, and difficulty managing his anger. He struggled with frequent visits from his wife's four sisters and felt they had the run of the house. He knew family was important to his wife, but he was her family too. He didn't talk about his feelings, the way his wife's sisters would. It left him feeling frustrated not knowing how to say how he felt. This would result in an outburst of emotion that his wife could never make sense of.

Harry's tendency to react with anger and demands for respect were influenced by past insecurities and a history of resorting to bullying behaviours. He had been brought up in a very controlled and repressed environment and talking about feelings or problems was usually greeted with a 'just toughen up' response from his parents. This upbringing made him into a very hard person with bad communication skills. Fast forward to his marriage and this had a detrimental impact on his relationship with Caitríona, leading to a lack of intimacy and affection when he was angry. Additionally, Harry's interactions and outbursts with his staff at work further exacerbated his anger issues, affecting his professional relationships. He was like a powder keg and the slightest disrespect would make him explode to show everyone he was boss. He had become an angry person because of frustration within and not knowing how to process inner turmoil. He had this belief that not being able to cope was weakness and feelings were weakness so he wouldn't process them. He believed that intimidation was the way to get respect – a trait he learned from watching his father. When he was growing up, he saw that other children had loving parents that hugged and played with them, unlike his own. He felt rejected and angry. His jealousy would cause him to lash out and bully the happy kids. He spent his whole life wanting to be needed and learned the destructive technique of demanding respect by intimidation. This was all to mask his insecurities that he had deep down.

The XYZ technique

Through coaching sessions, the XYZ technique was introduced to Harry. As discussed in chapter 1, this technique involved expressing emotions by filling in the blanks of 'I feel X because of Y, and Z would make things better'. It provided a structured approach to articulate his feelings and identify potential remedies.

His response in relation to his wife was: 'I feel angry and disrespected because you never listen to me when I say I want the house to be our home and not an open door. Having more family time of just us and the kids would help things.'

Old habits die hard

Harry was in a thinking loop that needed to be changed. These loops don't just change overnight, they take consistent work. Repetitious responses become habits. When you are triggered a certain way and you react the same way each time, this becomes a habitual response and you don't even think anymore, you just react. It is similar to muscle memory. This is why an angry or deeply unhappy person can appear to go from zero to a hundred in milliseconds when they are triggered. It has become a habit and practically automatic.

Like this:

EVENT Wife isn't listening to me ⟶ **TRIGGER** Harry triggered because he feels disrespected ⟶ **THOUGHTS** 'I won't allow you to disrespect me' ⟶ **EMOTIONS** Anger and rage ⟶ **DECISION** Decides to assert authority by demanding respect ⟶ **ACTIONS** Shouting, being harsh, intimidating, silent treatment ⟶ **HABITS** Becomes a habit over years ⟶ **BELIEF** This is how you get respect.

It is like autopilot. Our brain loves autopilot because it wants to conserve energy, and the more automated we can be, the less energy we use. This is why learning something new is so tiring at first, until repetition makes it easier. Approximately 40 to 50 per cent of what we do on a daily basis is done out of habit. For example, you get into your car and drive to work. You take a route you know well and have probably driven a hundred times. When you get there, you think to yourself, 'I don't even remember the journey.' You are so familiar with the route that you get there almost automatically. This is quite a contrast to the period when you were learning to drive – you were so aware of every click and clunk, getting the acceleration and clutch timings just right was an endeavour, especially when the handbrake was involved. Then you throw a hill start into the mix and it was exhausting. But now you drive and do it all without really having to think about it.

Our brain is wired primarily for survival. Part of that survival mechanism is preservation of energy and attention. If it felt like the first time you drove a car every time you drove, you'd be exhausted. Our brain learns things through repetition.

This is important as I want you to understand this principle. If such a high percentage of what we do is automated, that means, bearing previous chapters in mind, our habits are almost 50 per cent responsible for our mental and emotional state. Habits are not just what we do, but how we think and react. Almost half of the reason you are where you are in life is influenced by your habits, so they are definitely worth thinking about. These habits get formed by beliefs over time. We know that brushing our teeth is good, so we make it a habit. But like Harry, if we believe respect is gained by being intimidating, we subsequently form toxic habits.

Break a bad habit using a higher valued goal

Harry now saw that looking for respect highlighted his insecurities, and he had nothing to prove as a man. Most people don't want to change and will justify their bad habitual responses. But when you fully understand why you do what you do, you can look for a higher valued integral way of responding. This is when the reward for positive change is more valued than the result the bad habit brings. We now have an easy choice to make. Choose the higher preferred reaction as it will give us more internal reward.

STEP ONE: Identify that the reaction is wrong. Harry's reaction to being disrespected was wrong. His belief that everyone must respect him was also unachievable. He also believed that respect meant others submitting to him.

STEP TWO: Identify the origins. Why this reaction? Where was the root of this process? Harry's reaction was rooted in the insecurities he had.

STEP THREE: Create a new belief and healthier response. Harry's new belief was that he didn't have to prove himself to anyone. Lack of respect didn't make him any less of a man. No reaction was the reaction. He took a pause.

STEP FOUR: Cultivate self-awareness to help new actions. Give yourself daily reminders about this by reading about people skills and bettering your soft skills. Books like *How to Win Friends and Influence People* by Dale Carnegie were a huge help to Harry.

STEP FIVE: Keep track of triggers and events by journalling. Harry did this in order to identify the patterns that were not serving him well.

As you read this, take stock and look at your thinking habits, your reactions and the things that trigger you. Maybe they are old habitual ways of responding to an incorrect belief or even an outdated mentality. They need to go in order to make room for better habits. Keeping track of your habits is a great help; when you reflect on your week you can see if something threw you off a bit. Look at all the things you do habitually. Can you see any that aren't serving you well? I do this with clients who are trying to lose weight. For example, someone might get a takeaway and drinks every Friday. I don't tell them to quit the habit, but maybe to adjust it, like by having half a bag of chips. Is there a pattern of something that comes from a trait that doesn't serve you? Through journalling on your phone or in a journal we can then see the patterns and bad habits that are constantly tripping us up.

Decisions decisions

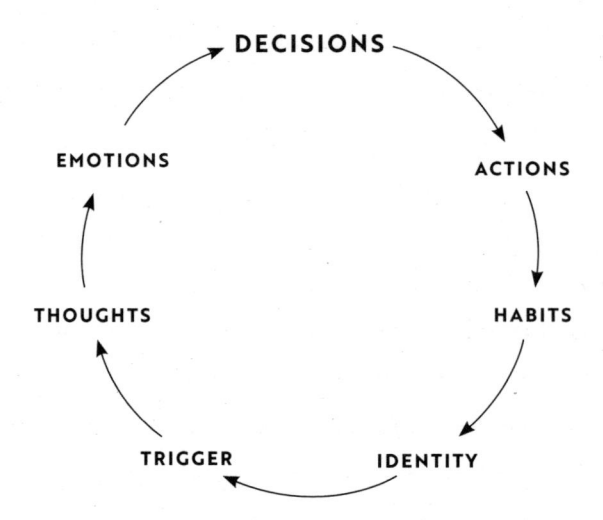

DECISIONS → ACTIONS → HABITS → IDENTITY → TRIGGER → THOUGHTS → EMOTIONS → DECISIONS

Every decision we make, whether it is good or bad, constructive or destructive, will have corresponding actions and outcomes. As we get used to making the same decision over and over, it becomes consistent and we create a habit. The habit isn't even thought about, it just is our response when triggered. In Harry's case, his destructive habit led to actions that others could see, so it was highlighted. But sometimes the habit is internal and cannot be seen by others. This is where I need you to be your own coach. I want you to pick one decision that you regularly make that you know is not the right choice. Perhaps it's a decision to avoid something you wish you didn't avoid, like a social setting. Or a decision to do something you wish you didn't do.

ONE-MINUTE CHALLENGE

Answer these questions.
- What regular habitual reaction do you have when triggered that disrupts peace of mind for you?
- What regular decision do you make that you wish you didn't?
- What would be a better decision?
- What stops you from making the right decision?
- Why do you allow this to stop you?
- What needs to be absent in order for you to make the right decision?
- What is the greater benefit?

I want you to start becoming aware of the decisions you make. You know the ones that are bad for you and have a negative result in your life. You don't need to dwell on the whole backstory to this bad decision, I just want you to grasp that there are decisions you knowingly make and probably don't admit at the time of the decision, which are bad choices. We all make bad decisions, but what one do you make on a regular basis that needs to change?

The people-pleaser example

What regular habitual reaction do you have when triggered that disrupts peace of mind for you?
I always try and please people when presented with the opportunity.

What regular decision do you make that you wish you didn't?
I wish I didn't people-please all the time.

What would be a better decision?
To go with my gut and say no when I want to. To respect my boundaries more.

What stops you from making the right decision?
I don't want to be rejected and crave acceptance to keep others happy.

Why do you allow this stop you?
I have grown up seeking acceptance due to low self-esteem and people pleasing helps me feel valued.

What needs to be absent in order for you to make the right decision?
If fear of rejection was not present and I had more confidence, I wouldn't people-please.

What is the greater benefit?
I will become someone who doesn't need approval, my self-confidence will grow. I will be happier.

THE F WORD

A word that is not a swear word but that people find very hard is forgiveness. Why should you forgive someone who hurt you or caused you pain and suffering? Isn't forgiveness only for the person when they are actually sorry? The reason forgiveness is so powerful is because it liberates you from the pain and suffering in your past. Let me share with you a story of a woman who came to me because she had held a secret for 20 years. We will call her Jessica. She had tried counselling and therapy but sadly it didn't get her the breakthrough she so desperately wanted. This secret had led to her developing severe anxiety. After she did my anxiety course, she reached out. I wasn't prepared at how candid she was as she shared the words: 'I was drugged and raped at a party when I was on holiday at 19. I never told anyone except for a couple of counsellors and therapists.'

Life coaches do not normally deal with cases involving trauma, but in this instance, I felt I could help.

We did about eight sessions and we dealt with the anxieties that reoccurred every day. Creating and building a new mindset became our work together. We did a lot of inner work on self-belief and overcoming fear. Fear was ultimately the driver behind most of her challenges. It was totally understandable how fear got into her life considering what had happened to her. She felt frustrated with herself for allowing this pain and trauma to haunt her for years and years. She was angry with herself that she could not let it go. But I shared with her that most people don't know how to deal with such an event, and that she had nothing to feel anger at herself for. She had done nothing wrong.

After her assault, fear came into her life like a roaring beast taking away her innocence and safety, and leaving a trail of pain and suffering for her to deal with. She was angry at herself for not being able to get over it and kept asking herself why she went to the party, why she was not more careful. All this anger at herself. We worked on her understanding that no matter what she did that night, it didn't give anyone the right to put a hand on her. Even if she chose to do drugs, get drunk and kiss every boy at the party, it was still not permission for anyone to touch her without consent. She was 100 per cent a victim and that was fact. She never reported the crime because she didn't know how to process it herself, and the shame of it kept her quiet.

She seemed so full of guilt, shame and anger towards herself. I asked her a question that made her break down: 'Do you forgive yourself?' I asked her if she forgave herself for internally beating herself up all these years because she felt somehow she was to blame when the truth was she did nothing wrong and was an innocent victim of a crime.

Through tears she said 'I know I need to.' This was the beginning of her healing. I got her to say it out loud even though she may not have meant it at first.

'I forgive myself'

Every time you go to be hard on yourself, say 'I forgive myself'.

This is liberating on levels you wouldn't believe.

Jessica was completely innocent of what happened her, but for others this is not the case. Perhaps something happened to you that you've blamed yourself for, maybe you even were partly responsible, or maybe you are fully responsible for what happened. Whether you were the victim or the perpetrator, if you are hard on yourself, mean to yourself or hurtful to yourself because of your past, I urge you to put the past behind you by uttering out loud the three words 'I forgive myself'.

I have worked with people who were fully or partially responsible for what they did. There was a person who manipulated the firing of a colleague through lies so that they could get their job, which eventually led them to be filled with guilt years later. Or the man who robbed people. Or the client who slandered their own sibling. I've worked with the victims and the perpetrators. If you acknowledge that you are the perpetrator of hurting someone and you feel remorse for doing it and take responsibility for it, then I can work with you, as you see the wrong in what you did.

Shame and guilt can show up for the victim, but they can also show up for the perpetrator who feels remorse. Shame is feeling bad about who we are. Guilt is feeling bad about what we've done.

If you feel either of these emotions, here is what needs to happen. Admit your failings and say aloud with your hand on your heart:

I give myself permission to forgive myself.

I give myself permission to let go of the guilt.

I give myself permission to heal.

To overcome shame or guilt we must forgive ourselves.

For Jessica, there was one more piece to the jigsaw. Jessica had never had a long-term boyfriend. She had an element of anger and fear towards men, but she also wanted to be married and have kids. We explored this and it was clear that she didn't trust men – which is understandable considering her horrible experience.

When the timing was appropriate, I asked her if she was ready to forgive her rapists. Now before you throw the book out the window, I want to explain how powerful forgiveness is. But before I do let me clarify.

Did these monsters deserve forgiveness? No. To forgive someone is not about whether they deserve it or not.

Is what they did a crime and should they have been charged? Yes. The law is for the lawless and forgiveness doesn't change that. You can forgive and drop charges, but you can also forgive and pursue prosecution.

Does forgiving them mean we are okay with what they did? No. Nobody should ever accept abuse in any shape or form, whether physical or verbal, and forgiveness does not mean you are accepting of this behaviour.

Does forgiving them mean they are off the hook? No. Absolutely not. Forgiving someone does not let them off the hook, it just means you are letting go of the pain they caused you. You are setting yourself free of the pain.

Forgiveness doesn't mean we let them off the hook, it means we let their hook off us.

When we have been hurt by someone in our past, it can haunt us. We can struggle to move on from it because every time we think of them or what they did, we practically relive it. We can feel all sorts of mixed emotions from anger to hate and even grief. Grief can show up because we may feel we have lost out in life. For Jessica, she felt grief because they took her joy, her innocence and her spark away at a time when everyone else seemed so happy. All those horrible images could come rushing back at the slightest trigger of a memory. When we have been hurt it is like the perpetrators have a hook on us, a power over us that they aren't even aware of. They have the power to hurt us as long as we hold onto what they did. Every time we replay it in our mind it is like them hurting us all over again. This can make us very upset, bitter, vengeful, angry and even hateful.

Pain is temporary, hurt is temporary, setbacks are temporary. But bitterness makes them permanent.

Bitterness is like drinking poison and expecting the other person to die.
NELSON MANDELA

Healing from the past

So many of us need the liberation of coming to terms with the fact that the past is the past; we can leave what happened in the past by breaking its hold on our lives through forgiveness. When we are stuck in our past, we tend to invest our time and energy by revisiting it. To withhold forgiveness keeps alive emotions of hurt, anger and blame which influence and distort our perception of life. Forgiveness liberates the soul. When we get to a position of being able to forgive, it is like soaring above the problem. The past is there, but you aren't there in it. You have set yourself free from it.

A higher value

Jessica had a breakthrough that made her realise it was time to forgive: it was her new understanding of what forgiveness would mean for her. The liberation from her past would be so valuable. What do you value more, understanding your past or building your future? Sometimes we don't get justice, sometimes we don't get the apology we deserve. The ego wants revenge, but we have seen that revenge won't heal you. You can waste your time analysing why, or you can forgive and look to your future. Jessica has now had a long-term boyfriend and as she puts it: 'I see my life like a garden. For 20 years it was just grass but now it has blooming flowers in it again.' That's the power of forgiveness.

Establishing what was most valuable to her was fundamental to Jessica's view of forgiveness. Forgiving meant freedom and disconnecting from the pain. Forgiving meant that she could stand tall and not feel shame. Forgiving meant that she accepted that what happened was not her fault. Forgiving meant that she could look forward.

EXERCISE
FORGIVENESS

STEP ONE: If you have caused hurt to someone, apologise to them

Bear in mind that just saying sorry doesn't mean that they will forgive you – it is for them to decide.

STEP TWO: Forgive yourself for the situation, whether you were in the wrong or not.

STEP THREE: After forgiving ourselves, we must 'forgive those that trespassed against us'. Forgive those that hurt you. This is where you will break free of your past.

STEP FOUR: Focus on the future and leave the past behind. A horrible thing happened to you but it won't define you. Again, this goes to identity.

How liberating is it when we get to a place in life where we can rise above those that try to persecute us? A place where we can stand up for ourselves and not allow others to influence our future negatively. That is what forgiveness brings. When you care less about persecution from others, you will find liberty. Will forgiveness be a part of who you are becoming?

Forgiveness is not a one-time event. It's a daily choice in the healing process.

CHAPTER 14

Financially stuck: money and manifesting

SHOW ME THE MONEY

One of the most common causes of feeling like a failure or feeling stuck is when we just don't have the financial freedom we desire. The temptation to compare our financial status to that of our peers can leave us disgruntled. Is there anything we can do when we feel stuck on the wrong side of the tracks financially? I don't give financial advice, but I will be sharing how you can get financially unstuck and how it starts with us.

Here are two of the most important questions you can be asked about your financial future:

1. Have you found the opportunity that's going to take care of you and your family for the rest of your life?

2. Are you spending some time every week looking for that opportunity?

If you answer 'no' to the above two questions I hope it stopped you in your tracks to contemplate at the very least the power of that no. Put it like this: if you said no to both questions you are saying, 'No, I haven't found the opportunity that's going to take care of me and my family, and no I am not looking for one.'

Seek opportunity and you will find it.

I'm not highlighting this for you to feel bad, instead I hope it gives your instinct a nudge that perhaps you need to start looking. We all have different backgrounds and I know what it's like not to be born with a silver spoon in your mouth, so to speak. When I was born my parents didn't have a home, so we lived in a caravan in my granny's back garden for a number of years. I know what it is like to struggle financially.

My parents grafted and eventually got their own home. I had a happy childhood. We were happy with what we had at the time, and that's the key. But it is also important not to limit yourself from increase and growth.

It is okay if you haven't found the path to support you financially, but to not be looking for it is a concern. When you start looking, you start to give yourself opportunity. One of the greatest things you can give yourself is the belief that change is possible.

Asking yourself the right questions is fundamental to creating the positive change that you crave for your financial situation.

This applies not just to a person's personal life but also to business. When a company finds itself stuck, hitting a ceiling in performance or losing its status with customers, is it on the right path? If not, is it looking? Sometimes we feel stuck because of our previous success. We try to do what we did before, only now times have changed and the old way may not work. Blockbuster and Xtra-vision used to be the way to rent films to watch at home. That was the number one way, until things changed and streaming became the new number one. If we are stuck, maybe it's because we aren't looking to create new opportunities. Maybe our old ways of winning need to be upgraded. We get stuck when we believe there is no other way, so we stop looking.

POVERTY MENTALITY: SUSAN'S STORY

When Susan was 17 she left school and started working in the beauty industry. Over time she grew to love what she did and she was also very good at it. Never one to sit still, her career was everything to her. Eventually she got to the most senior role in the company and her instinct to start her own business was calling. The most influential person in her life was her mum, who always supported her, but when it came to the conversation of starting her own business her mum couldn't fathom the concept. 'Are you mad?' her mum would say. 'Think about the security you have in your job now, and they love you there.' Susan put it off more and more until, inspired by another woman's success story, she finally made the decision to go for it. This shows us again how the people we surround ourselves with can help or hinder our potential, even the people we love dearly.

Imposter syndrome

A few years passed and Susan's business became very successful, and then she came to me. She heard about a programme that I run around mindset and coaching for business owners that focuses on performance coaching. She wanted to be more focused and grow her business and her team even more, but she was struggling. She was struggling with imposter syndrome. Imposter syndrome is when you feel you aren't able for the role you are in and are like an imposter, it can also be feeling not worthy of the role due to comparing yourself to others more qualified in similar roles. She wanted advice and tools to deal with her anxiety around this because she was now in the spotlight due to her success. She thought to herself, 'What if I make a mistake and it comes crashing down?' and 'What if my mum was right?' All these fears and anxiety circled around in her head leading to sleepless nights of worry that had now started to overshadow her life.

She reached out to me when an online thread had been started all about her and it was filled with hate. People were writing things like 'the bubble will burst', 'who does she think she is?' and 'what qualifications does she have?'

I knew that she must have dealt with gossips before, so I asked her why this suddenly triggered all this fear? We chatted some more and it came to light that her mum was always putting fear into her, dating back to when she started to work for herself. She would say things like 'Oh, that's a lot of responsibility', 'I know a guy who lost it all' and 'There is no security when you work for yourself'. Over and over again, when Susan would start something or achieve something, her mum would cast a shadow of fear. Susan was used to this, but now that she had got to a level of financial success that even she found daunting, fear crept in. Her mum reinforced it, and the thread online basically grew this fear into a monster. Anxiety and the 'what if' fearful questions started rolling through her mind. What if it all comes crashing down? What if I can't cope? What if my anxiety gets worse and I can't function?

Susan was falling victim to scarcity mindset. This is a mindset that there isn't enough to go around. Years ago, scarcity mindset was also referred to as a poverty mindset.

Scarcity mentality is a mindset that basically says:

- Spending money is bad.
- Money can only be spent on necessities, not treats.
- Opportunities are limited and rare.
- Success is temporary.
- Avoid all risk.
- Success only comes once, if at all.
- Remaining at the back of the pack is safest.

It often comes from an upbringing where there was lack and things were sparingly given out. This upbringing can reinforce a poverty mentality. If a parent has this mentality, they will teach their child their ways whether they mean to or not. Their ways condition the child, and the fear of not having enough is so strong that a person won't invest or spend, instead saving their money and taking no risks. People with this type of mentality won't take risks like starting a business or investing in marketing. They avoid financial risk, storing up what they have and seeking to get as much as they can.

Susan didn't have a scarcity mentality, but everyone around her did, so it had a huge influence on her. There is a big difference between handling money with wisdom and handling money with fear. Poverty mentality sees having some extra money as bad because there is an association that if you have money, you are an evil person or have notions. I see this a lot when people from tough backgrounds who may not have had much grow up. They tend to think that people with money are bad people who are out to get you. They have a belief that money might make you evil. I have seen some people's religious beliefs convince them that having wealth is somehow unholy and being poor is closer to holiness. This mindset can be very limiting to one's life and financial future. Greed is not healthy, but wanting to be successful is.

Yes, there are bad people with money, but there are also bad people who have no money. Limiting beliefs around money can cause a person to get very stuck and conditioned to a level of income. In doing so, they cut off their potential in life. Money is not evil, but the greed for it is. Wanting more is not bad, but how you go about obtaining it might be. Why not wish for yourself to be as successful as possible? Why limit yourself and your income? Why fear having wealth if you are fortunate enough to be able to have it? People think that money changes people. It can, but so can not having money.

In a research study carried out by Thomas C Corley, over 200 self-made millionaires were interviewed and asked about their beliefs and attitudes about money.[7] He found that a common thread among these millionaires was that they did not have a 'poverty mentality', proving that this mindset is certainly not financially advantageous.

I worked with Susan on her self-esteem and self-belief by using the circles exercise from chapter 3. I also introduced her to other business-minded people in my membership group called Tribe. Having like-minded people around her and dealing with limiting beliefs was key. It was upwards from there.

A sad person without money will still be a sad person with money

I've worked with people who actually fear having money because they worry about it changing them, or they worry about losing it all. So, they put themselves in a position in life and career to stay at a level that feels safe. It is something that people don't like to talk about, but when I talk to clients you would be amazed at people's negative views on money, wealth and having nice stuff. Greed is not right as we all know. The 'why' behind wanting to make money is important. If your intentions are good in nature and it won't cause hurt to others to earn money, then this is the way.

For Susan and many others, I shared with her that pursuing your passion and purpose needs to be your drive and if you can make a few euro doing it, then great. If pursuing your passion makes you a millionaire what is wrong with that? After years of working hard Susan became very successful and now shares her story with those she meets. She is always quick to tell them that if scarcity mindset had taken hold, her potential would have never been realised.

Side note: true success should never be measured by monetary measures, but instead by the fulfilment life gives you. Realistically, most people won't become millionaires, but that does not mean they can't be wealthy. So, when I talk about wealth, this is my definition: true wealth is when we are fulfilled in what we do and we love the life it allows us to have. That is true value in life and you don't need a million euro in the bank to have that.

BECAUSE I'M WORTH IT

Then there are those of us who feel that they aren't deserving of being wealthy. They feel that they don't deserve it because of where they are from, or imposter syndrome might tell them that they aren't able for this level of income. For some, when they come into a new level of income, it can bring fear. This is because having a significant amount of money is unfamiliar. It is not about the exact increase, but sometimes more to do with the principle of receiving an increase.

Often a person will say to me, 'I don't feel I deserve to be wealthy.' It is a limiting belief that is more common than you think.

I usually reply with, 'So you deserve to be poor? If you have a child and you love them, would you tell them that they deserve to be poor? Of course you wouldn't, so why believe it for yourself?'

Self-worth

Self-worth is how we value or appreciate ourselves. Self-worth is internal, and having healthy self-worth is knowing that you deserve to be treated fairly, knowing that you are good enough, you deserve to be loved and your potential in life is the same as everyone else's. I have seen people not wanting to get a promotion or win at something because their low self-worth tells them that they don't deserve it. This is a very common reason for people getting stuck in life. They don't want to raise their head and be noticed because their self-worth is so low. They don't feel worthy of wealth. Wealth is a bonus, but it's a travesty to believe that you aren't worthy of it. Every human being deserves the best in life and if they are lucky enough to be well-off financially, this is a blessing, not a curse.

EXERCISE
90-SECOND EXERCISE

Ask yourself the following questions:

Do I have a low self-worth? If so, why?
Example: Yes. I feel I wouldn't be able to have extra money or even deserve it.

Does this impact career/business decisions?
Example: I tend to not go for promotions. I play things safe.

What action can I take to work on this?
Example: I will explore why I feel this way and start journalling to identify when I get tempted to feel this way.

Self-sabotage

The fear of having money has subconsciously caused people to lose it all. I know a family personally who came into a windfall with their business, only to self-sabotage and lose a lot of it because they didn't know what to do with it. The challenge of making money was solved and this new playing field was so foreign that they self-sabotaged in order to go back to being their old selves, who they were familiar with. I had one particular client who had a belief that when he had good fortune in business, it meant that something bad would happen – a total limiting belief. So much so that he told their accountant to not tell him their profit but instead only let him know when there is loss. He felt more relaxed when there was a loss in a quarter than a profit. For some reason, profit made him feel guilty and fearful, so he would quickly give it out as bonuses or squander it (I am sure his staff didn't mind). You may not even realise you are doing it, but you might form an untrue belief that more money will change you, so end up getting rid of it. This is self-sabotage rooted in fear.

PASSION OVER PROFIT

If you are stuck financially, one of the greatest investments you can make (which costs very little) is to invest in you – ironing out any and all of the quirks you may have around money. Self-belief is the catapult that can bring you to the position you wish to obtain, whether that is working for someone else or working for yourself. Things can hold us back and these can be mind blocks and bad habits that may be partly the reason we are stuck.

In chapter 4 we discussed how to create a mindset and outlook that will help rather than hinder you. You can achieve the income you desire if you tune your mindset in, listening to those that can encourage you. Of course, it takes hard work, but it is better to be busy trying to get there than to be idle, wishing you were there already. Get specific in your goals, get a plan in place and start leaning into your financial future. But please be advised, whatever you want to do in life whether you are 21 or 61, pursue passion over profit. That is what leads to fulfilment. That is the real wealth in life.

Pursue passion and profit will follow.

It is so tempting to blame everyone else for our financial position: the government, the economy, our upbringing, teachers, even where we are from. Yes, they all have a bearing on how we fare, but the responsibility for whether we stay stuck or not is in our lap. You might have gone through situations that cost you – I totally accept that. But if you get into the habit of BSE (Blaming Someone Else), you get stuck there. Instead, become passionate about the future you want. Visualise how you want your future to be and start to plan for it.

Think big with small steps

If you want to make more money, ask yourself, 'What could I do today to make €10?' Then with that in mind, could you do it 10 times? That's €100. Now what if you increased your price to €20 and did it 20 times? That's €400. This simple little example makes approaching your finances easier, with bitesize, actionable steps. If you want to go on holiday this year and need to make €2000 more, that's about €38 extra a week. Perhaps looking at your bills, asking for a raise, starting a sideline job or getting a financial advisor would give that to you.

Don't just look at the big figures, break it right down and you will find it easier to see where the extra can be found. If you can't see it, then look at getting professional help, it is your future after all.

VISUALISATION

Visualisation gets misrepresented in the spotlight today and is sometimes talked about as if it is a magic process. 'Think it and you'll have it' is a common ideology that unfortunately is not true. A more accurate truth is that thinking and action create opportunity. This is not just from a financial perspective but applies to everything in life. As we have discussed, how we see ourselves is who we become. We have an image of who we are and what we are capable of, and it is this image that lights the path we are on. If we feel we are worthless, we illuminate the proof of this belief. If we believe we have purpose in life, our mind will illuminate the evidence to back this up, as well as the opportunities that give us a sense of purpose.

Visualisation is like an anchor. These visualisations are the internal images we imagine and set for ourselves as goals. They are like the satnav for our potential and accomplishments.

Imagine you already are the person you long to be. Now imagine what you need to do today to become that person. This will help you to form new habits. It is a lot harder to quit on your journey when your decisions have become new healthy habits.

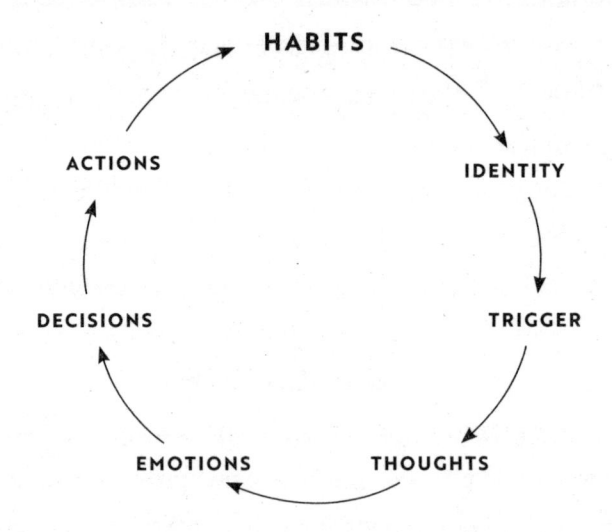

```
        HABITS
   ↗            ↘
ACTIONS      IDENTITY
   ↑             ↓
DECISIONS     TRIGGER
   ↖            ↙
 EMOTIONS ← THOUGHTS
```

Arnold Schwarzenegger tells the story of how he saw a movie as a boy in the early 1960s called *Hercules*. Something in him gravitated to the strong man that played the lead role. Arnold, a skinny boy living in Austria, felt something within him stir. 'This is who I want to be like,' he thought to himself. Photos and magazines of strong bodybuilders littered his bedroom walls as he started to learn and train to become this herculean man. He ultimately became a world-champion bodybuilder and even met Lou Ferrigno, an actor who had played Hercules in another film. They became friends and Arnold exceeded all his expectations, even becoming bigger than Hercules.

Then acting called and he applied the same technique of visualising, learning and focusing on the action heroes he wanted to be like. His accent and bad English became his trademark rather than his weakness. Arnold became one of the greatest action heroes of his time. Then politics called. Again he set in motion the same routine, and a few years later he became governor of California.

Being foreign in the United States, having bad English and not knowing American culture were all hurdles that stood against him, yet he succeeded. This was not just because he visualised it, but because he put the hard work in. His peers would say that nobody trained harder than Arnold. He became obsessed with his focus. He had setbacks, he made big mistakes, but he never gave up. I share that story because it is evidence of how having a visual as an anchor, whether it is tangible or just internal, is very important. Putting the work in is vital to manifesting the dream. You can't think yourself to success.

When manifesting fails

When you sit down to plot and plan what you desire in life, whether it's personally, professionally or relationally, you must also write down what potential hurdles might be currently holding you back, as well as the potential hurdles that might crop up. Studies have shown that when we envision potential challenges, we deal with them better if or when they show up. It's kind of like you are half-ready for it. It is solid preparation. Many people give up on themselves because they feel that life happens to them rather than for them. True, there is a lot we cannot control, but we still define the direction.

When I work with a company, the easy part is defining the goal, then we define the strategy. But a lot of my work goes into discussing the weaknesses that might hold the company back, as well as what problems we foresee. Fail to prepare, prepare to fail. Don't just visualise who you want to be, visualise the hurdles so that you can prepare right now for them and set yourself on a trajectory for success.

Just like when you're building muscle, you need to have SMART goals and steps that allow you to observe growth. Science has shown that when we seek out progress, it creates a sense of achievement, no matter how small it might be. This reinforces our commitment to the process and actually spurs us onwards.

Visualisation, goal achievement and manifesting is about intentional planning, thoughtful execution and setting realistic expectations. It is seeing clearly in your mind and heart what it is you are working towards.

But remember, you must incorporate aligning your goals with your values in order for your dream to be authentic to you. After we have set the destination, it is about taking consistent action towards achievement. Correct visualisation requires seeing the process. Actually seeing yourself doing what you need to do, as well as the end achievement, is true visualisation. No magic trick, just clearly defined direction and consistent work in alignment with your goals to get there. The result is that it tunes your mindset in to seeing opportunities that may help you, it influences your decisions, actions and habits, ultimately defining your identity and who you become. It is proven that dancers and gymnasts who visualise themselves doing their routines before they do them actually perform better, almost like muscle memory. You are showing your brain what you want to achieve.

If you imagine yourself as a failure, you will create that identity for yourself. You have the power to see yourself as a success or a failure, that decision is made by you. Whatever has you stuck, pause to create an image of how life will be when you are unstuck.

Now let's look at the steps you can take daily to get there.

EXERCISE
CHANGE YOUR FINANCIAL POSITION

When you are passionate about something because it brings you a sense of fulfilment and purpose, it is that thing you need to go after. Perhaps you want more time off but need to earn a certain amount. Maybe you want to get a promotion. Get clear on your desires. Anyone successful will tell you that when you pursue your passion, profit will eventually follow. I will also add that if you aren't happy with the position you are in financially in life you don't have to stay there. If you hate a job today imagine how low it will get you if you are still there in five years' time. Start dreaming of what you want.

1. SMART Goals

   Be clear on what it is you want **Specifically**. How progress can be **Measured**? Is it **Achievable**? Is it true to your values and **Relatable**? Plot a **Time** for achievement.

2. Visualise your future

   Read about others who have done what you want to do. Seek out people like this who you can talk with. Get into the mindset of the person you need to be to accomplish your dream goal. What hurdles do you need to prepare for?

3. Define daily small steps
Start with small steps that you can take consistently to create healthy habits.

4. Get the numbers
Even if you have no idea where to start, get your figures and speak to a financial advisor who can make the money you have work smarter, not harder.

5. Cultivate the growth mindset required
Deal with any limiting beliefs that contradict how you visualise yourself becoming. Edit and replace them with the belief that you can achieve what you desire with hard work and a plan. Define the beliefs or affirmations you need to have in order to get there.

Money is a tool and never your master.

CHAPTER 15

Spiritually stuck: finding true happiness

THE TWO GREATEST FORCES

The two greatest forces in humans are love and fear. Love shows up in many forms. It can be love of another person, a goal, or ourself. It can be love of what brings you fulfilment. It can be love for life, love for what you do, love for happiness. Being kind is love. Being selfless is love. Love is a force, but so too is fear.

Wherever love and fear show up, there is a choice. It is this choice that decides which path we take, whether it is for love or for fear. Therein lies the key to getting unstuck and becoming unstoppable. Viktor Frankl, a psychiatrist and holocaust survivor, realised that whether we understand it or not, we have a choice and we are choosing a path every day. The following quote is often attributed to him:

> **Between stimulus and response there is a space. In that space is our power to choose our response. In our response lies our growth and our freedom.**

There is an incredibly powerful resource that we can tap into, which is life-changing when discovered. I discovered this inner part of me, and it changed everything. I would liken it to when a drilling company taps into an underground oil reserve and it explodes onto the scene, then it is piped off and becomes a constant source for when you need it. This inner power resource is something you are already aware of, and I will show you how to activate it more often than perhaps you do already. It is the decision-making part of you that knows what you truly want. I had seen glimpses of it throughout my life, but it wasn't until one of my darkest times that I could identify it as clear as day.

This resource is having a **survival instinct**. I put it another way: It is a deep desire for your life that says, 'I won't give up.' It is the instinct to hold on to hope with the belief that you will manage to get through this challenge somehow. It is faith.

Love versus fear

We all know what love and fear are, but I am going to share the meanings of the words so that you understand what I mean when I talk about them.

LOVE: an intense feeling of deep affection.

FEAR: an unpleasant emotion caused by the threat of danger, pain or harm.

Fear is an unpleasant emotion, and it can manifest in different ways for people. When we feel stuck, it can be because fear is at the helm of our decisions. Identifying what exactly it is we fear is a good start to overcoming the fear. When it comes to decisions, for example, we have an unpleasant feeling because we see that there is a right and wrong decision to make and we fear making the wrong one.

For example, a conversation with a client might go like this:

'Mark, I'm not afraid or fearful, I just don't know what to do with my career.'

'Have you tried anything that you think you might like to do?'

'No, because I am so confused about what I want.'

'Is there any reason why you haven't tried to do anything?'

'Yes, what if I try something and it is a waste of time and I hate it?'

It may not seem obvious, but fear is controlling their decision. They believe that wasting time is a failure and time is to be valued. They fear going against their belief and value, so they don't make a decision. Risk is dangerous and it feels unpleasant, so they avoid risk in order to avoid failure. Fear is at fault. This is a limiting belief stemming from a fixed mindset that doesn't see that risk can actually pay off.

The one who avoids failure will also avoid success.

If you don't try anything new, you remain stuck. You might believe that you don't fear failing, it is just you don't want to fail. The truth is that failing would make you feel unpleasant because you see the risk of failure as negative. Parents and school probably taught you this (failure is to be avoided; don't fail that exam, for example). It also feels like you let yourself down if you failed. You are not in a fearful state of trembling about the decision, but you are in an avoidant state – avoidance of a decision because the potential good outcome is not guaranteed. Avoidance and doing nothing are a choice, just like taking action is. For all of the above reasons you stay stuck, take no chances and avoid risk, all because you fear what might happen.

Is there an action that you are you putting off due to risk that could also be the first step towards your solution?

Sometimes figuring out what you don't want is easier to do than knowing what you do want. You see, it is not a failure to try new things and take risks, it is all learned experience. Seeing failure as something to be avoided is actually a limiting belief and a trait of a fixed mindset. Nobody wants to fail, but if the primary motive in life is to avoid risk, then you won't learn or grow much.

HEAD AND HEART

Envision yourself as consisting of three interconnected parts: your head, your heart and your body.

Your head

The head is the decision maker. It's the place that has intellect, imagination and thoughts. It can be rational and irrational, in a happy or sad state, and is the place we all are familiar with. It is essentially the mind. Forty to fifty per cent of what we do on a daily basis is habit, but the rest of what we do is choice. You are in control of it for the most part – but not always, as the mind is always assessing things consciously and subconsciously.

So where does the real you dwell? The mind can sometimes think things we would rather not think, it can also get distracted when we don't want it to. It can give us nightmares in our sleep when we would rather avoid them. So clearly, thoughts are sometimes in our control and sometimes not. Where is the part of us that knows what we want to think and what we don't want to think? There is another part to us that coexists – the decision-making part. There simply must be a final decision-maker to know what we like and dislike within our thoughts.

Your heart

See your heart as the true you, the real you. Your heart is the part of you that instinctually decides, almost without rhyme or reason. It just knows. If I asked you whether you remember ever making a decision that worked out contrary to what the facts would have you do, you can probably agree that the heart gets it right most times, if not all the time.

Your heart, or your spirit, is the very essence of who you are. Some people might think your spirit and soul are the same thing. They are not. Your soul is comprised of your mind, will and emotions. Your soul is the part of you that decides what to do and can stop your heart from doing what it knows it wants to do. This is the real battle – when your soul and spirit clash, or as I say, your head and your heart. Think of yourself like three circles.

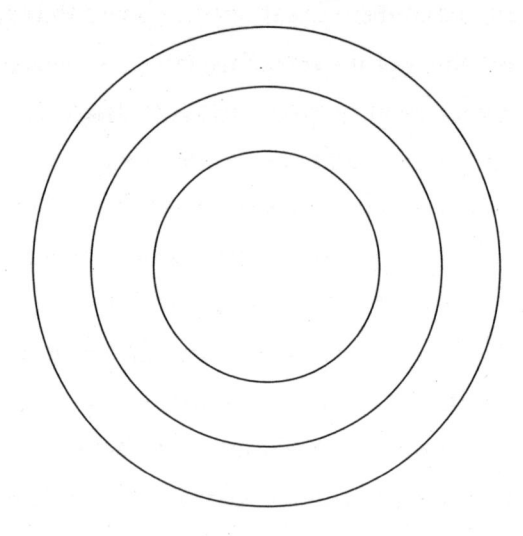

The outer one is the body, the inner one is the soul and the core of you is your spirit. Your spirit basically is the true you, your core. But let's keep it simple and say your head and your heart.

Your heart always knows but never shouts – your head thinks it knows and only shouts.

Paul's story

Paul went to Trinity College Dublin to study medicine with the hope of becoming a doctor: an expensive and arduous task costing a small fortune, paid for by his parents. His parents always pushed him towards this profession because his dad was a doctor and it made sense in their minds.

Paul was in his sixth year of college and the little voice that said 'don't do this course' in year one was now a thunderous roar. His real passion was painting and art. His head said what his parents' heads said: 'It's a great career with financial rewards, become a doctor.'

But his heart loved art. He wanted out of this course. Ultimately, he came to the conclusion to put his studies on hold and embrace his painting, which he had always done on the side with any spare time he had. His parents were devastated and not one person supported him. But he owed it to himself to try it for a year.

He chose his heart over his head. He shared how he felt so much joy every week of pursuing his passion. He struggled as an unknown artist and began a business restoring furniture and painting it. But his intrinsic why, to work at his passion and succeed, led to him building a highly successful business in restoration alongside his art business. His pieces hang on the walls of many very fine homes. He would tell you that pursuing your passion and listening to your heart is the only way to be truly happy. With that, I agree.

TRUST YOUR GUT INSTINCT, THAT IS THE REAL YOU

Your heart is your gut instinct but is also your compass. It tells you every day what you should do and what you should avoid. One time Fiona and I were selling a house and I met a couple of sales agents to see who we wanted to sell it for us. I went with the one who had the flashy brochure and all the promises, and on paper looked the best.

But my gut had said to go with the other salesperson, even though I had no other reason than my instinct. I went with my head, so I chose the flashy one because on paper he made sense. We soon realised I had made the wrong decision and he failed miserably. I was faced with a decision – do I let this guy continue to try, or do I eat humble pie and go back to the other agent. My ego could feel the pain of it, and it could have stopped me, but I have learned that the ego rarely does what's best for you. I did a U-turn and went back to the agent that my heart wanted me to go with. She turned out to be brilliant.

Listen to your heart, it knows what we don't see.

What does science say about trusting your gut?
Researchers at the University of New South Wales ran a study in 2012 which was published in the journal *Psychological Science*.[8] The researchers set out to examine the role of intuition – our gut instinct – in decision-making, and whether the brain could accurately predict the outcome of a choice before it was consciously made. They used a series of visual tests and brain imaging techniques (fMRI) to analyse brain activity during decision-making.

The participants in the study were shown a series of images, and they had to make a decision about which images they preferred. The researchers found that activity patterns in certain regions of the brain could predict the participants' preferences up to 11 seconds before they consciously made their decisions. Their gut instinct knew before they even consciously became aware.

This study suggested that the brain was unconsciously processing information and forming preferences before the participants were even aware of their choices. In other words, their gut instincts or unconscious intuition were at play and could predict their decisions more accurately than their conscious thought processes.

Values are constant
Values, when established, are constant, meaning that they are always running in the background when decision-making happens. Decisions that don't impact values happen all the time, but our gut reacts to decisions that threaten or could impact our values. But what gets in the way of our gut instinct is sometimes too much information. It is like when you are trying to decide between two things online and you scan through to compare the pros and cons of each. Your gut says you want to pick the right one, but your head can't decide due to information overload. What happens in that instance? A study from 2011 may have the answer.

In 2011, researchers from the University of Amsterdam conducted a study that investigated whether unconscious, intuitive thinking could lead to better decision-making than our conscious, rational thinking.[9] The study, led by Ap Dijksterhuis, was published in the journal *Science*.

Participants were presented with information about four different cars. Some participants were asked to consciously analyse the information and make a decision about which car they believed was the best option. Meanwhile, other participants were distracted with an unrelated task, preventing them from consciously analysing the car information. Afterwards, they were asked to make a decision without having consciously thought about it.

The results of the study showed that participants who relied on their unconscious, intuitive thinking (those who were distracted and prevented from conscious analysis) made better decisions than those who engaged in conscious deliberation. The participants who relied on their gut instincts had a higher likelihood of selecting the best car based on the information presented.

This study suggested that sometimes conscious overthinking and analysis might hinder our ability to make the best decisions.

By tapping into our unconscious, intuitive thinking, often referred to as gut instinct, we may be able to arrive at better choices, particularly in situations where the decision-making process is complex or involves a large amount of information. We can just make a choice rather than risk overthinking and making the wrong one.

Values interact with instinct and so being led by them usually results in finding the path that is in alignment with you. This is why diving deep into your motivations is so fruitful, as it can unearth the things we truly value and identify those things we thought we valued but give us no return.

EGO

There's one obstacle that often prevents us from following our hearts over our heads, and that obstacle is our ego. The ego encompasses a person's self-esteem, self-worth, and self-importance. While it's healthy to have positive self-esteem, the ego can become negative when it derives its sense of worth from belittling others or comparing oneself to others. It's important to understand and control the ego, as it needs regulation. Ego is the part of you that becomes the problem when your identity clashes with expectations. For example, when someone angers you, the old you (your ego) says 'How dare they!' and you let them have it. The new you that you want to be (your identity) says, 'Don't react until you've calmed down because you might say the wrong thing and regret it.' Here are some examples:

- You see yourself as a person with integrity, which is good (identity), but ego gets riled up when others don't see that fact.
- You see yourself as successful, which is good (identity), but ego says that due to this success you are better than other people.

Your identity is who you are and how you see yourself. Ego however wants everyone to know who you are and reacts when someone doesn't. A person is wrong for feeling superior and acting egotistically, just as feeling inferior and acting with a lack of confidence is not healthy. The goal is to see ourselves as equals to others. However, if our ego craves attention and recognition, it's okay as long as it doesn't come at the expense of ourselves or others. Ambition is a positive trait, as long as it is motivated by the right reasons. Striving to be our best is commendable, but only if it doesn't harm or undermine others. Winning is desirable, as long as there is no hatred towards the opponent.

I've witnessed people who desperately want to be seen, and their need for recognition ends up destroying their lives. They achieve what they desire, but through means that their hearts would never approve of. There are those who cheat in exams because they desperately want to excel academically. There are teams who aim to win so badly that they create false stories in the media about the opposing team's star player to unsettle them before a match.

The ego manifests in various ways, and it's not inherently evil. However, we must constantly keep it in check. It can lead to unhealthy behaviours, like not asking for help because your ego is too proud; or wanting to start a business but being held back by the fear of failure and the judgment of others. We might become people-pleasers because our egos crave popularity, even though our hearts sometimes want to say no.

Our ego pursues what it wants rather than what is best for us. It prefers comfort over discomfort. It desires an easy path without putting in the necessary work. The ego yearns for respect without wanting to earn it. But if we feel we earned respect, the ego will demand even more of it. Yes, everyone deserves respect, but the ego will make it an emotional problem for you when respect is not given. It acts as a spiritual barrier, residing in our heads. The ego wants things even when they are morally wrong. The ego says leave the gym until another day. The ego says you deserve to have that cake, you've worked hard enough.

How then can we distinguish between what is right and wrong for us? What is good and bad? The part of us that knows what is right and wrong is our heart. It is the part of us that loves. The heart is generous and giving rather than self-centred. The true reflection of our inner self is when we do something that may seem illogical but serves a greater good, like acts of generosity. The ego, on the other hand, often impedes generosity by asking, 'What's in it for me?'

Doing the right thing doesn't always mean you win. Doing the best thing doesn't mean it's best for you.

The most challenging thing about our ego is the fact that it looks out for us, not others. We can get stuck when we spend our lives trying to get even, trying to get recognised or trying to win all the time. Winning in life is only truly winning when it was your heart driving you. Ambition and a desire to be the best is perfectly healthy for the right reasons, provided it doesn't cause you to deny your heart or hurt others.

Head/ego will lead you to believe:
- That mistakes are pain.
- That failure is bad.
- That you should complain in order to get heard.
- That you are a victim of life.
- That risk is to be avoided.
- That it is acceptable to lie to protect yourself.
- That it's about being right.
- That image is everything.

Heart/spirit will lead you to believe:
- That mistakes must happen in order for you to grow.
- That failures are necessary lessons.
- That there is enough for everyone, generosity is good.
- That constructive criticism is good.

- That you are a victor of life.
- That risks aren't bad.
- That you should take accountability for actions.
- That it's about what is right, not who is right.
- That image is what you think of yourself, not what others think of you.
- That people leaving you has made space for better people to come in.
- That hurt people hurt people, and you won't allow hurt to make you bitter.

From the stories throughout this book, you can see parallels to how the head and heart react. When we are stuck we must learn to listen to our heart, our gut instinct for it is our very spirit that knows what to do. It may not have it all figured out but it will know the next step. Being led by our hearts is being led by our true self, our true rightful identity. It is like a muscle that must be worked. It gets better and stronger the more we decide to listen to it as opposed to the noise of our ego. Let me use respect as an example. You deserve to be respected and treated accordingly. But if you are not the ego reacts. But a better way that leads to freedom comes when you stop caring what people think. Yes, speak up and don't be a doormat for someone to walk over, but also care less about what they think, focus on protecting your peace. The ego will cost you your peace if left in charge. What leads you?

I mentioned how love is a powerful force, and as we all know, so is fear. What leads you in your life as you go about your day?

Love encompasses more than just the affection we feel towards a child or the romantic love we experience in a partnership. It extends to the profound appreciation we have for life itself when we discover our purpose and what truly brings us fulfilment. Love reveals itself in the things that hold value, meaning, and affection for us. Love is the ultimate superpower, and those who embody it are the true superheroes. Love emanates from the heart, not merely the mind. While it is true that we can experience love in our minds, such as the love for chocolate, a good movie, or a holiday, the love I am referring to is much deeper, selfless, and fulfilling. It is a love directed towards the things that truly matter in life. It is that love that needs to lead you, and that love comes from deep within you. That love needs to be what moulds your identity and who you become.

Fear is so powerful it tells you:
- You can't.
- You don't have what it takes.
- You can't make it work.
- You're a failure.
- You aren't enough.
- You're unworthy.
- You don't deserve to be happy.

The difference between the fear narrative and the love narrative is the truth. Love tells a true story, for love shows you what you need to do in order to feel fulfilled. Even if love is saying start that business and even if the business fails, the key is you went with your heart, no regrets, lessons learned, onto the next adventure. Fear tells a story that you won't make it so don't even try.

Love has a very different story. Love says:
- You can.
- You have what it takes.
- You can make it work, and even if it doesn't, you'll be stronger for it.
- You're a survivor.
- You are enough.
- You are worthy.
- You deserve to be the happiest you can be.

Most of us don't think with our hearts, we think with our heads. We lose ourselves and our potential amidst the fog of limiting beliefs and the inner critic. But we all have the power to choose whether we are led by our head or our heart, and we can make that decision starting right now.

I don't need your help

The ego hates to ask for help and even hates the fact of admitting the need for help. I've had clients so upset and frustrated within themselves because they couldn't fix something and hated the idea that they needed help. They viewed asking for help as a failure. It is a limiting belief of the ego to presume you have all the answers to every problem you encounter in life. When we listen to the ego and refuse help, it is like locking ourselves in a cage with our problem. Don't let the ego lock you in a cage with no help. The ego can isolate you and even make you think there is no help that will work, because to be vulnerable is not something the ego likes to be.

ONE DEGREE IS ALL IT TAKES

Two planes take off from an airport and as they dial in their heading, one plane puts in just one degree more than the other plane. They will take off and be heading in the same direction for a long time. However, 10,000 miles later the planes will be located thousands of miles away from each other. That one degree of difference at the start results in a huge difference over time.

I want you to start cultivating a self-awareness that oversees how you speak to yourself. When you make decisions, ask yourself:

- Is this my head or my heart speaking?
- Is this love or fear?
- Is this love or ego?

The changes might feel small. If you wouldn't speak to a best friend like that, then don't speak to yourself like that. Take the heart and love approach to your life. It feels like nothing at the start, but as you lean into this better way of living, in time that one degree change will have you on a new course to a happier you.

It can help to write things down. Look at decisions you've made in the past, and ask yourself if you were being led by your head or your heart. This can help you to identify a pattern. Journalling can help us to take stock of how we are but also why we are. Am I like this because I let my ego win out? Am I like this because fear made me decide?

When we live by our heart we start to live a life true to us. It is there we find fulfilment.

CHAPTER 16
The road to fulfilment

INSTINCT AND IDENTITY

Our past, our financial situation, our relationships, traumas, hurts, failures: all these things will try and tell you who you are. Society, siblings, parents, teachers, bosses and the government will all try it. The ego will try to tell you who you are, and that you deserve this or that. The truth is that all these things are influences, and if you are unhappy with how things are, it is changeable. Who do you say you are?

I never thought I could get over anxiety, as all the influences told me it was a futile dream. But I did overcome anxiety all those years ago. It was never a problem again and I've helped thousands of people do the same. I had society tell me I could never be happy if we didn't have children, and although we would love children, not having them didn't mean we couldn't be happy. True, there was sadness, but I chose to not set up camp there. I listened to my heart, to my instinct, accepted what we could not change and leaned into what we could. I worked on who I needed to be, the person I saw myself as; my identity of being fulfilled by helping others achieve the same. A happy person is content on life's path even when detours come up. They are grateful for what they have as opposed to focusing on what they don't.

I accepted some dreams would not come true but that doesn't mean I stopped dreaming.

I never thought we could be happy again if having children of our own was taken away. But I thank God that happiness did return. Trusting my gut instinct that as a couple we would get through this together and accept what is was the same approach that rescued me from the grips of anxiety. Getting clear on how we saw ourselves being in the future, being a couple happily in love – this became our identity and reality.

Being your best true and authentic self comes from accepting the things you cannot change, working on the things you can and pursuing what your heart desires. A lot of our happiness and peace is within our control, and as we have seen over the course of this book, our quality of life starts and ends with how we see ourselves: our identity. The triggers will come and go, but the action you take, the direction you go, the responses you will have, will all be ruled by your identity and how you see yourself.

The true values you will hold – like love, integrity, peace, kindness and strength – will be your very essence. The beliefs that you are valuable, you are worthy of joy and happiness, and the belief that you are enough, will flow through your heart. Everything starts and stops with who you are today and the incredible person you are becoming. Set your identity and the reality will follow.

FREE IS ANOTHER WORD FOR UNSTUCK

You are free to make the rest of your life into whatever you want it to be. Nobody can stop you from living life on your terms. Pursuing your dreams and goals needs to be a priority. Life is so short and goes by so fast, but remember that you are free to enjoy it. It is about living a life that makes you feel content. A life that puts a smile on your face. Life won't always treat us fairly, but reassure yourself that even in your toughest storms, you're going to be all right; that's the power of hope. Develop that deep understanding that you are valuable, you are deserving of love, peace and happiness. In fact, you are pretty incredible. You weren't born for no reason, and you are meant to be here. Every day, even if it is for just a moment, include the things that bring love and peace into your life. You are in control of your life, not other people, not your past, not your fears.

ONE KEY IS GRATITUDE

Research has shown that being grateful for who you are and what you have is proven to benefit your emotional well-being. Value this gift we have called life and never take it for granted. When you start to be grateful for the life you have, you start to love it again.

But you also start to love yourself. Not in an egotistical way, but in a way that recognises that you are worthy of a blessed life and you deserve a blessed life. For you to have simply survived the womb is a biological miracle, let alone the incredible feat of navigating life and being here today reading this. Loving life again starts by being grateful. Start with the little things. Many people would trade everything to be where you are in life.

Be grateful for what you have survived: the bad people, the awful situations and the traumas of life that you managed, somehow, to get through. Maybe you are still healing, but you are here, which means you survived. You are a victor. When you live by your heart you start to live a life true to you, and it is there you find fulfilment. Forcing ourselves to create a habit of gratitude influences how we feel, and it is available to use whenever we need it, first thing in the morning and last thing at night.

Realise that you were destined to be a successful, happy, blessed person. The road is not a straight one but there is a road, there is a destination for you to walk towards. It is called fulfilment. Knowing that your identity is routed in how you see yourself and what you chose to value is fundamental to reaching your full potential in life.

It is never too late to start, but starting is what you have done by reading this book. This was the first step; there are more steps to take. It might be slow, but nothing is slower than the person doing nothing. Connect with me online, and get support. Seek out your tribe and find like-minded people. You're more than welcome to join our online Tribe or the workshops available. Your potential is ready and waiting to be tapped into because you aren't stuck, you are breaking through. The future has not yet been written, but the pen is in your hand.

You won't just be unstuck, you will be unstoppable.

Acknowledgements

I have been to that place called rock bottom and I thank God that it was the making and not the breaking of me. To have a best friend, supporter and wife all in one person is truly a blessing, and she has been by my side through thick and thin. I can't let the book close without thanking the woman I love, my Fiona. I would not be what I am today if it weren't for her love and support.

Thank you to my family, who have been so supportive. My mum and dad gave me so much wisdom and advice that it still echoes in my heart when I coach people today. Thank you to my mum for always encouraging me to be the best and to my dad for always having the right words at the right time when I needed them. I can attribute a lot of my own identity and self-belief to my parents and I thank them for that and their love. Thank you to my sisters and their families for supporting me all the way.

I must also thank two women who aren't with us anymore but were hugely influential in my life: my grandmothers, Nanny and Ma. They were so different in character but taught me so much from a young age. Nanny was so calm and pleasant, right up to her last days as cancer took her life, she had an unwavering faith in God and was a lover of life and books. I definitely inherited her reading gene. Ma, who had so much hardship, sickness and death over her lifetime, still knew how to laugh and be happy and always had incredible advice. Her resilience and strength were incredible. My grandparents were like my coaches in many ways as I grew up with their wisdom.

I have met many amazing people throughout my career both personally and professionally and I want to say a thank you to each and every person that helped support me and the work of coaching people that I am so passionate about. I am excited for what's to come because, as I always say, the best is yet to come.

Endnotes

1. Kirkebøen, Geir, and Gro H. H. Nordbye. 'Intuitive choices lead to intensified positive emotions: An overlooked reason for "intuition bias"?' *Frontiers in Psychology*, vol. 8, 2017, https://doi.org/10.3389/fpsyg.2017.01942.
2. Merzenich, Michael M., et al. 'Brain plasticity-based therapeutics.' *Frontiers in Human Neuroscience*, vol. 8, 2014, https://doi.org/10.3389/fnhum.2014.00385.
3. Locke, E. A., & Latham, G. P. (2002). 'Building a practically useful theory of goal setting and task motivation: A 35-year Odyssey.' *American Psychologist*, 57(9), 705–717. https://doi.org/10.1037/0003-066x.57.9.705.
4. Langer, E. J., & Rodin, J. (1976). 'The effects of choice and enhanced personal responsibility for the aged: A field experiment in an institutional setting.' *Journal of Personality and Social Psychology*, 34(2), 191–198. https://doi.org/10.1037/0022-3514.34.2.191.
5. Acevedo, Bianca P., et al. 'Neural correlates of long-term intense romantic love.' *Social Cognitive and Affective Neuroscience*, vol. 7, no. 2, 2011, pp. 145–159, https://doi.org/10.1093/scan/nsq092.
6. De Quervain, Dominique J.-F., et al. 'The neural basis of altruistic punishment.' *Science*, vol. 305, no. 5688, 2004, pp. 1254–1258, https://doi.org/10.1126/science.1100735.
7. Corley, Thomas C. *Rich Habits: The Daily Success Habits of Wealthy Individuals*. Itasca Books, 2010.
8. Lufityanto, Galang, et al. 'Measuring Intuition.' *Psychological Science*, vol. 27, no. 5, SAGE Publishing, Apr. 2016, pp. 622–34. https://doi.org/10.1177/0956797616629403.
9. Dijksterhuis, Ap, and Zeger Van Olden. 'On the benefits of thinking unconsciously: Unconscious thought can increase post-choice satisfaction.' *Journal of Experimental Social Psychology*, vol. 42, no. 5, 2006, pp. 627–631, https://doi.org/10.1016/j.jesp.2005.10.008.